S0-BAM-253

110-119
149-158

BY THE SAME AUTHOR

SANCTITY

The Path to Perfection
The Pure in Heart
The Secret of Radiant Life

HOMILETICS

The Approach to Preaching
The Craft of the Sermon
Power in Preaching

APOLOGETICS

Give God a Chance

DEVOTIONAL

Why Jesus Never Wrote a Book
He is Able
God Does Guide Us
These Things Abide
Ten Statesmen and Jesus Christ
Let Me Commend
Teach Us to Pray
They Met at Calvary
etc.

WESTMINSTER SERMONS

W. E. SANGSTER

WESTMINSTER SERMONS

VOLUME TWO
At Fast and Festival

LONDON
THE EPWORTH PRESS

FIRST PUBLISHED IN 1961

© THE EPWORTH PRESS 1961

Book Steward
FRANK H. CUMBERS

252v
Sa58
V.2

143435

SET IN MONOTYPE BASKERVILLE AND PRINTED IN
GREAT BRITAIN BY THE CAMELOT PRESS LTD
LONDON AND SOUTHAMPTON

For
MARK
PAUL
PAULA
and
PETER
With Grandpa's love

Foreword

THESE SERMONS form the last work of William Sangster. They were sent to the publisher only a day or two before he died. Nor will there be any more, for, though he left over a thousand manuscript sermons, their author left also the wish that none be published after his death.

The last weeks of his life were spent correcting and re-writing these sermons. He was virtually helpless, retaining only a little strength in two fingers of his right hand with which to hold a pen. His voice had long been lost, and his only means of communication left with those he loved and with the world was his pen—and therefore this book.

Yet the finest sermon he ever preached is not in this collection, though the book tells something of it. That distinction belongs, not to any he preached from the pulpit, nor to any printed word, but to the last years of his life. It was then that Dr Sangster preached his best, and preached, curiously enough, in silence. And now, except for this last book, the rest also is silence.

P. E. SANGSTER

Preface

IT WILL HELP the reader of this book if he reads the Preface to Volume I. He will learn there how I came to be publishing sermons at all, and how I selected them.

This series of sermons deals with the chief days (and periods) of the Christian Year, and with days of the Church and Calendar Year which call for special notice in the pulpit.

As one who has written on the craft of homiletics, I still regret that the sermons asked for are not more exact illustrations of the homiletic 'types' I have distinguished in *The Craft of the Sermon*, but it may be with preaching as it is with medicine. My friends in general medical practice tell me that they seldom meet a case of sickness precisely as the text-book sets it down. They can identify its main features, but each sickness has some of the personal peculiarities of the patient in it too. 'True to type' doesn't mean exact duplication.

It may seem like playing into the hands of the cynic to compare sermons and sicknesses(!) but this similarity is there. At the last, the test is not the purity of the homiletical type but whether it did the work.

I have to thank again—and I do so most sincerely— the Rev. Greville P. Lewis, B.A., B.D., for reading and commenting on the sermons, Miss Margaret Gregory for typing the MS. and Miss Marie Berry for reading the proofs. Without the loving help of home, none of the work could have been done at all.

W. E. SANGSTER

LONDON, S.W.18

Contents

1. *Advent:* HE IS COMING I

2. *Christmas:* HE IS HERE 10

3. *Year End:* HE IS MASTER OF TIME . . . 18

4. *Year Beginning:* HE MAKES ALL THINGS NEW . 28

5. *Lent:* HIS DESTINATION IS IN HIS FACE . . 37

6. *Passion Sunday:* HE IS LONELIER THAN THE LONELIEST 47

7. *Palm Sunday:* HE HONOURS AN ASS . . 57

8. *Good Friday:* HE DIES. HE *MUST* DIE . . 65

9. *Easter:* HE RISES AGAIN 74

10. *The Forty Days:* HE TARRIES AMONG US . . 81

11. *Ascension:* HE MOUNTS IN TRIUMPH . . 90

12. *Pentecost:* HE POURS FORTH THE SPIRIT . . 101

13. *Trinity Sunday:* HE SHARES SOCIETY IN THE GODHEAD 110

14. *Children's Sunday:* HE HAS A SPECIAL LOVE FOR LITTLE CHILDREN 120

15. *Youth Sunday:* HE CONFIRMS THE COMMANDMENTS 129

16. *Harvest Thanksgiving:* HE DELIGHTS IN OUR GRATITUDE 138

17. *Overseas Missions Sunday:* HE CLAIMS THE WHOLE WORLD 149

1

He is Coming

*Isaiah 9²—The people that walked in darkness have seen a
great light*

NO INFORMED person today will deny that the
human race walks in darkness. The awful pall which
followed the blinding flash of the atomic bomb when it
burst above Hiroshima has spread across the world, and
the shadows are not fully dispersed even yet.

Peace-making discussions on armaments, and atomic
power, have proved disappointing so far, and none of us
is completely quiet in mind or ready to describe the
present state of the world as 'peace, perfect peace'.

Many competent observers, not normally given to
pessimism, despair of our race and half suspect that we
are not only a people who walk in darkness but a people
who walk in darkness to their doom.

And so we come to Advent Sunday and to this pertinent
word: 'The people that walked in darkness have seen a
great light.'

What is Advent? What makes it the beginning of the
Church year?

It speaks to us of both the advents of our Lord: the first and
second—though it is with the first that I want to deal now.

It is the first gleam of Christmas; it is the promise of
His coming; it heralds the entrance of the Divine into
human history; it is heaven descending to earth; it is a
great event casting its brilliance before it.

It is as though a trumpeter had taken his stand upon the turrets of time and announced the coming of the King. 'Get ready', he seems to say. 'Get ready. He is coming.'

What a message. Welcome at all times, it is doubly welcome now. The King is coming!

> Let every heart prepare a throne,
> And every voice a song.

Now why do I say that this message, welcome at all times, is doubly welcome now?

Because for years men have been seeking to organize human life without God. They have tried to thrust Him out of the universe which He has made. For years they have laughed at the preacher and told him to drop his silly patter about redemption. They have said that man has no saviour but himself.

'If we must have religion,' they argue, 'it must be a religion without revelation—a religion of humanity and not a religion of God.'

Walt Whitman was their poet. He said he loved cattle and all dumb beasts because they did not kneel down and say their prayers!

W. E. Henley was another of the same breed:

> Out of the night that covers me,
> Black as the Pit from pole to pole,
> I thank whatever gods may be
> For my unconquerable soul. . . .
>
> It matters not how strait the gate,
> How charged with punishments the scroll,
> I am the master of my fate:
> I am the captain of my soul.

The vanity of it! The master of his fate and the captain of his soul!

And so, because these critics found it hard to believe in God, they transferred their faith to man. They invented (in the middle years of the last century) that strange creed of positivism—the worship of humanity—and Walt Whitman said:

'Glory to man in the highest.'

'The difference between the old artists and me', he said, 'is this. They painted one head with a halo of gold-coloured light about it, but I give a halo to all.'

The years went by and this worship of our human nature grew popular because it fed our conceit.

It was nice to be told that there was no truth in the old doctrine of original sin; in fact, that there was no sin at all—just a bit of selfishness which time would correct; that the Golden Age was inevitable and that, by gradual steps, man would move unaided to perfection.

I say it flattered the egotism in us. It made redemption unnecessary. It emptied the Cross of meaning. It made the Church a joke. All this chatter about being 'born again' was nonsense. As cars got faster men got better. The path to the heights was plain.

And then we woke up! First in 1914, and then again in 1939, we found ourselves in hellish war. The mid-years of the century find us still unsure of peace. This, then, is the perfect world we had been promised by the men who sneered at original sin; a world of atomic submarines, air-raid shelters, gas-masks for babies, guided missiles, and hydrogen bombs.

A world of television, plastics, possible trips to the moon—but also the possibility of radiation poisoning, and mass death! The incredible folly of it; the ignorant conceit; the puffed-up egotism!

Is it not obvious now to everyone that unredeemed man, neglectful of his Maker, takes the path to the pit and would make this fair earth a gory hell?

What can we do except call back the King?—summon again to His rebellious world the banished Monarch, and crown Him Lord of all?

And that is part of the Advent message: 'The people that walked in darkness have seen a great light.'

The ancient seers of God in times of national peril strained their eyes through the darkness and caught the gleam. Let us look ahead ourselves and descry the essential meaning of His incarnation. Something wonderful is impending in Heaven. Let our adoring hearts run out to meet Him and cry with Charles Wesley:

> *Come Thou long expected Jesus,*
> *Born to set Thy people free,*
> *From our fears and sins release us,*
> *Let us find our rest in Thee.*

And now let us contrast the lot of those who have Jesus as Guide and Saviour and Friend, with those who still ignore those outstretched hands and think that man can save himself.

It doesn't matter whether we think first of our *problems*, our *sorrows*, or our *sins*. Without Jesus, we are a people walking in the darkness; with Jesus, we are a people walking in the light.

I

Think, first, of our problems. Who are we? Why are we? What is this human life? What is the *meaning* of it? Where is it leading to?

Schopenhauer, the distinguished German philosopher, who spent half a life-time brooding on the mystery of existence and never could make up his mind who man was and why he was here, was sitting one day in the Tiergarten in Frankfurt when the park-keeper, disliking his dishevelled appearance and thinking him a tramp, accosted him and said: 'Who are you?'

The philosopher, interrupted in his reverie, looked up and said with awful earnestness: '*I wish to God I knew.*'

That is the dilemma of the humanist. He doesn't really know what to make of this strange human nature. He has no answer if you say: 'Who are you?'

Nor are we better off if we turn with the same question to a modern philosopher like Bertrand Russell. He has pondered deep on the problems of human existence and he has no other answer than his: 'You are an eddying speck of dust; a harassed, driven leaf.'

If you seek from him and his kind the meaning of life, they say: 'The *meaning* of life? There is none really. No doubt we could make our brief existence a little better if we tried.'

Or if you ask for light on what follows when this life is past, they say, with Sir Arthur Keith: 'Nothing follows. Life goes out like a guttering candle.'

They walk in darkness, and they do not see a great light.

So I turn to Jesus and the apostles, my hot, impetuous questions falling from my lips. I will ask *them* who I am, and what is the meaning of life, and what comes after this; and there is an answer for every question.

'You want to know who you are?' says Jesus. 'You are dear to God, and dear enough for me to shed my blood.'

'I can tell you,' says Paul. 'You were bought with a price.'

And John breaks in: 'Beloved, now are we children of God, and it doth not yet appear what we shall be.'

'What is the meaning of life, Lord?' I ask. 'What am I in the world *for?*'

Plainly He answers: 'To seek, first, God's kingdom and His righteousness.'

'And, Lord, when the fever of this life is over, what then? What follows for us mortal men and women?'

He smiles and says: 'In my Father's house are many mansions. If it were not so I would have told you. I go to prepare a place for you.'

There it is. Plain dealing with plain questions. Light in darkness. The fruit of His coming. Is it any wonder that when we think on our problems we are thrilled with Christmas anticipations, and say from our hearts:

> *Come, Thou long-expected Jesus,*
> *Born to set Thy people free.*

II

Or, if I turn from my problems to my *sorrows*, I find it just as dark among those who deride religion, and just as bright about my Lord. I turn to the purveyors of religion without revelation; the people who believe that we can save ourselves, and say: 'I am in deep trouble, I have lost a dear one.' Or: 'I have suffered the heaviest reversals in my financial affairs.' Or: 'I have learned the gravest news from the doctor.' Or: 'I have been cruelly dealt with by a man I thought my friend.'

I pour out my heart to them, and they say: 'Well, you must cultivate other interests.'

Fancy saying that to a man who has lost his wife: 'You must cultivate other interests!'

Or they say: 'You have just got to put up with it'—which one knew already, but craved for a crumb of comfort in the meanwhile.

Perhaps they answer: 'We have all been through that, and you must take your turn with the rest.'

Nor do some of them conceal their conviction that they never made half the fuss about it that you are making.

And if I go farther and expose to them my very heart;

if I say, 'I dread the thought of this hydrogen bombing. The more I dwell on all that happened in Hiroshima and Nagasaki, the more unequal do I seem to what may happen here', some of them say: 'Cheer up, it may never happen. Besides, some of the bombs may be duds!'

And that is all! Little chips of worldly wisdom; a flickering match struck in the dark. They do not know. They have not seen a great light.

So I turn to Jesus.

'Lord,' I say, 'I am in trouble——'

And before I can go farther, He says: 'Come unto me all ye that labour and are heavy laden and I will give you rest.'

'Lord,' I continue, 'I will keep nothing back. This hydrogen bombing haunts me. Have You no word for me in these dread times in which we live?'

And He says: 'Work for disarmament but, in the meantime, "be not afraid of them which kill the body and after that have no more that they can do".'

'But, Lord,' I protest, 'suppose everything is lost. Some say that civilization cannot be salvaged and that we have come to the end of the age.'

And He smiles and says: 'Fear not—it is your Father's good pleasure to give you the kingdom.'

III

Or, if I turn from my problems and sorrows to my *sins*, He is still my Helper and Saviour, and there is none other than He. If I turn to the humanists with my sins and guilt, they can barely restrain a smile.

'Nobody worries about their sins today,' they tell me. 'There is no such thing really. A bit of the beast survives in us, and traces of selfishness—but not sin! Sin is a Jewish taboo, and a Victorian convention. Don't bother about it.'

B

'But I *do* bother about it,' I insist. 'I have an unquiet conscience and an unclean heart. I feel soiled inside. This is deeper than any disquietude a man might feel in breaking the social code. Can you do nothing about my sin?'

And they can do nothing about it. 'Forget it', they say. 'Just forget it'—and leave me in the dark of hopelessness. They do not see, and cannot make me see, any light.

So I turn to Jesus, and the moment I come into His presence I cry: 'Depart from me, for I am a sinful man, O Lord.'

And He says: 'Be of good cheer; thy sins are forgiven thee.'

A coroner held an inquest in Paddington recently and publicly reproved a doctor for the neglect of his duty.

It seems that the doctor had been attending a man suffering from acute asthma, and had given him a series of hypodermic injections in the chest.

When he was giving him a fresh injection, the needle broke. The doctor wanted to remove the needle, realizing the danger, but the man said: 'Leave me alone. I feel too ill. It won't matter.'

So the doctor left him alone, and unhappily the needle pierced the patient's lung, and he died.

There are many people who talk like that about sin. The humanists do. They say: 'There is social conduct and unsocial conduct, but not sin. Drop the word. It is just a hangover of superstition. It doesn't matter. Leave it alone.'

But it does matter. It is inside us and it strikes at our vital life. There is death in sin—but life in Christ.

That is why we exult in the message of Advent, and that is why, despite the encircling gloom, there is a song in our heart and a spring in our step as our Church year begins again.

We have seen a great light. In Christ we have the answer to our *problems*, our *sorrows*, and our *sins*. He is equal to them *all*.

> *O come, O come, Immanuel,*
> *And ransom captive Israel.*

2

He is Here

John 1[14]*—The Word became flesh, and dwelt among us*

DR STANLEY JONES has told a story of a little boy who stood before a picture of his absent father, and then turned to his mother and said wistfully: 'I wish Father would step out of the picture.'

That little boy expressed, in his own way, the deepest hope of the deepest souls who lived before Christ.

They believed in God! Socrates and Plato did—the finest of the Greeks. The ancient Eastern sages did: Gautama, the Buddha; Lao-tze, the Chinese teacher; Akhnaton, the most profoundly religious of the Pharaohs. With overpowering intensity the Hebrew prophets did: Isaiah, Jeremiah, Ezekiel, and all the rest of them.

They believed in God! They believed that God could be seen in nature. He had made the world. In many ways, it was a picture of Him. Indeed, the most daring of them rose even to believe that the great Creator of the universe might be called a Father.

The psalmist said: 'Like as a father pitieth his children, so the Lord pitieth them that fear Him.' They got as high as that—but farther than that they could not go. In their heart, this longing, I fancy, could easily have taken shape: 'I wish the Father would step out of the picture.'

You see? They were saying, in effect: 'I wish that the Creator could become real. Real to us!'

Stars are lovely to look at—but they can't *love*. Flowers are beautiful—but they have no heart. It says in the florists

window: 'Bouquets and Wreaths.' Either! The flowers
don't mind. They will come to the wedding or the funeral.
It is all the same to them. They are beautiful, but
they are not personal. The mountains are majestic, but
there is no comfort in their cold hearts.

Oh for a warm heart in the Universe! If only the
Father would step out of the picture. . . .

Listen! Listen! HARK!

He *stepped* out of the picture. He stepped out at Bethlehem. Here is the glorious truth of it: 'The Word became
flesh and dwelt among us. . . . No man hath seen God at
any time; the only begotten Son, which is in the bosom
of the Father, He hath declared Him.'

Christianity is not just a religion of influences and
values and principles. It is a religion of happenings; of
events; of plain historical occurrences. Indeed, the faith
is based on such. It belongs to the very marrow of the
Gospel to assert that God came at a certain hour in
history, and at a certain place on earth; lived and died
among us, and afterwards rose from the dead.

The man who says, 'I cannot believe that. I admire
the ethics of the Sermon on the Mount, and much of
the teaching of Christ, but the historical part of it I
find incredible'—that man might be many splendid
things, but he could not be a believer in the Christian
religion.

The Christian religion carries certain facts at its
heart, and the greatest of them is this: 'The Word became
flesh, and dwelt among us.'

We have come again to Christmas-tide. Christian
teachers have long insisted that, if the central truth of
Christmas be grasped, we have the answer to all our
deepest dilemmas. Is that true? If the Father has stepped
out of the picture, do we not know the true nature of the
world, of *God*, and of *ourselves*?

I

Christ's coming tells us the true nature of the world.

What a world we live in! So many conferences seeking to secure enduring peace break down. We seem utterly incapable of rising to the concept of world federation. We seem insanely bent on taking the path that leads to division, and, it would seem, ultimately to war.

And if, in our survey of the world, we turn from the follies for which man himself is responsible, and look at the world of created nature—how strangely mixed it all is.

The man who sees nothing but little puppies, and lovely sunsets, and scented flowers, and mother-love, is not looking at the *whole* world. He is repeating Nelson's device without Nelson's excuse. He is putting his telescope to the blind eye whenever he comes to something he doesn't want to see.

We are not of that number. We hold the faith in the face of all which seems to contradict it, and we recognize again how strangely mixed is the record of nature.

Think of the way that stoats deal with little rabbits. Remember that it seems to be in the nature of stoats *so* to deal with rabbits. What a horrible picture that conjures up in your mind!

Think of the way a cat will deal with a half-dead mouse. Remember again that it seems to be of the very nature of cats *so* to deal with a half-dead mouse.

Think of the way that lampreys live—if you have any interest in those strange creatures at all. Remember how, with their scale-less bodies and sucker mouths, they rasp off the scales and flesh of living fish and eat them alive. What a repulsive picture it conjures up in the mind! Think of the soldier-ants of South America, which move in their millions, nearly an inch long, with enormous pincer jaws which pull their victims apart. Remember how they pour like tar over every living thing in their path. One recoils in horror from each recollection of it.

It seems, at times, less like God's world than the devil's world; or, as though God, having made it, left it, or even —terrible thought!—had been excluded from His own world by some malignant enemy. What is the truth about the world? When one studies it in detail, and looks at it whole, what emerges from a patient scrutiny of physical nature, and of life as man has organized himself upon the earth?

Listen! This is the message of Christianity. Let it stagger you if it will, but do not be in any doubt as to what it is saying. It is saying this. Whatever seems to contradict it, this is the world God visited to redeem His people. It is not the devil's world, nor yet really man's world; it is *God's* world. Rebellious—admittedly—but still His!

Sin cannot ultimately defeat Him. The idea of some automatic human progress (which warmed the heart of our Victorian fathers) may be impossible for us, but this world is still *God's* world.

Be sure of it by going again to Bethlehem. In all the growing madness of things; in the frustration and bitterness of the hour—come and pause by the manger and hear the truth of your most holy faith. This Baby is Almighty God. He will grow and struggle with this world, and, as He leaves it at the last, having lived the perfect life for our example, this He will say to all who care to listen: 'Be of good cheer; I have overcome the world.'

II

Not only does this great divine event tell us the truth about the world. *Christ's coming tells us also the true nature of God.*

You see, the awful thing about studying the world of nature, and the world of warring men, is the thoughts it arouses concerning the character of God.

Of course! That is always the important thing at the last. If I were a pigmy in the heart of Africa, and suddenly transported by plane to an operating theatre in a London hospital, I might draw the very worst inferences from what I saw.

Imagine me standing in a corner and seeing a human being brought in and laid on a table in a state of nature. Imagine that I observed him put to sleep before my eyes, and then saw the doctors and nurses come in with masked faces, and picking up knives begin cutting open that prostrate body. Suppose I saw the blood spurt and that inanimate form slashed about in front of me—what would I, as a pigmy from the heart of the African forest, be able to infer from it all? It would seem to me like some ghastly ritual murder; some evil, ancient practice which my own tribe had abandoned years ago. It would seem to me that I was witnessing something satanic and awful in the extreme.

But if it was explained to me that, despite all the appearances to the contrary, a kind purpose lay behind it all, that not death but life was the aim; not evil but good the motive; not 'pain inflicted' but 'pain removed', the purpose of it all—if I was *sure* of it—O! that would make all the difference. Not just *what* was happening, but *why* it was happening, and the high purpose in it would put all my fears to rest.

And when I look at the world, that is the big question still. I study nature, and I study the relationships of men, and, as I study, I know that the biggest question is not just what is happening, but *why* it happens; what it is telling me about the nature of the Universe as a whole; what it is disclosing concerning the main purpose at the heart of it.

The biggest questions I pose to my mind are these: Is it all Chance behind the Universe?—a blind, unreasoning fate?—or is some satanic power in charge?

Am I, and millions like me, the pawn of impersonal forces; an unconsidered trifle in this vast purposeless existence?

Those are the most solemn questions: not atomic warfare; not bacteriological warfare; not rockets, nor poison gas, nor travel in space, but whether, despite all that seems to contradict it—the knives and the blood and the masks of this vast operating-theatre—there is a holy purpose at its heart, a meaning which redeems it all.

The Christian faith answers that. Be staggered again if you must by the answer, but do not be in any doubt about it. Your religion says that this Jesus, whom all intelligent people admire and concerning whom even some unbelievers say, 'His was the peerless life', your faith says that this Jesus was 'the express image of God'; God Himself; 'the image of the invisible God'; the One who, when Philip said 'Show us the Father', answered: 'He that hath seen me hath seen the Father.' 'God manifest in the flesh. . . .' (All these are the actual quotations of scripture!) 'No man hath seen God at any time: the only-begotten Son, which is in the bosom of the Father, he hath declared him.'

III

The truth about the nature of the world.

The truth about the nature of God.

Finally, *Christ's coming gives us the truth about ourselves*.

I do not know how it is with you, but I will be frank and say that, whenever I meditate on myself, I am brought very soon to depression.

There is such a contrast between the man I want to be and the man I am. So wide a gulf divides the ideal of holiness I carry in my heart and my meagre achievements. Even when my deeds pass my scrutiny, my motives don't.

How much have I ever done for the pure love of God?
I come to the year's end and I look back over my past
New Year resolutions, solemnly made, earnestly pursued,
but O! so seldom achieved. I see that I am a strange being
really, with something of largeness built into my nature,
but more of littleness coming out; with longings to be clean
through and through, but covered in stains.

I often wonder, as you must do: 'What is the truth
about myself?' What—in the language of the theologians
—is the real nature of man?

And then I come to Bethlehem—and move to Nazareth,
and to Capernaum, and follow Jesus through His lovely
life. Here I see the man I ought to be.

So my longings after holiness are *not* an illusion! It
happened once. A Man, who was tempted in all points
like as I am, lived that life. It has been done. It shines
through all the ages. Many who do not believe that He
was God believe that there was no man like this Man.

Is this, then, the truth about myself? I concede that
there are senses in which, as I dwell upon His moral
triumph, I only deepen my own depression.

But only momentarily.

What I most feared was that I was incapable of good, a
bit of earth, and nothing more. I see now, for all my
failures, *that* is not true of me.

Proverbial wisdom says that you cannot make a silk
purse out of a sow's ear . . . and I have often suspected
that that was my true nature. 'A bit of a swine' (as the
man in the street might say); a sow's ear incapable of
conversion to anything better, and finding my natural
food in the pig's swill.

But He comes and will not let me believe it; puts His
hand on my shoulder and says: 'You do not belong to the
piggery. You belong to me!'—stoops and lifts me from
the dirt and tells me that He loved me enough to forsake

the Courts of Heaven; did not abhor the virgin's womb; came as a Babe and lived this life to show me how it could be done; stretched Himself on the wood at the last, and died to redeem me.

Is that the truth about me? Was I dear enough for God to be *born*? Was I dear enough for God to *die*? Let no man tell me now that I am worthless; the creature of an hour; the fruit of my parents' sexual passion, and nothing more.

Let this Christmas story be true and nothing else matters. The Father *has stepped out of the picture*. I have the truth about the world. I have the truth about God. I have the truth about myself.

> *Yea, Lord, we greet Thee,*
> *Born this happy morning;*
> *Jesus, to Thee be glory given,*
> *Word of the Father,*
> *Now in flesh appearing:*
> *O come, let us adore Him, Christ the Lord.*

3

He is Master of Time

2 Corinthians 6² — *Now is the acceptable time*

I

ALL OUR LIFE we have been the slaves of time. If it were not prostituting the most solemn metaphor we know, we might speak of half mankind as crucified upon a clock. Time, time, time has dogged us like a demon since our tenderest years.

Cast your mind back to childhood and recall how you were haunted by time. What were the most hateful remarks we ever heard as children, and heard every day? 'It's time to go to bed', and then: 'It's time to get up.'

My mother complained about me, as no doubt your mother complained about you, that I was so contradictory in that I never wanted to go to bed, and contrariwise I never wanted to get up.

I heard a psychologist say once that any man could have a will of steel if, every day of his life, he would just do two things he didn't want to do.

It is nonsense, of course. All my life I have been going to bed and getting up, but I wouldn't say I had a will of steel.

Nor does this enslavement to time end in childhood. Our bondage becomes closer with passing years. When the cry fades from our ears, 'Time for school', 'time for homework', 'time for music practice', it only gives way to another form of time-slavery. Time for work! A more insistent clock. Longer hours. The minutes so important now that many people are even compelled to 'clock on'.

Do you clock-on at your work? When you feed your card into the time-machine and pull the knob, do you ever want to smack its smug, conceited face? He has no bowels of mercy, no pity, has the clock.

He cannot record that it was a bit foggy, or that the bus queues were longer, or you were especially tired that morning.

'You are late', he says. 'Ten whole minutes. I'm going to tell on you.'

And 'ting' goes the bell, and you have 'lost' a quarter of an hour.

You company directors who are here know nothing about that. You don't clock-on in board-rooms. But even *you* know the imprisonment of time; racing from engagement to engagement; fitting this in with that; giving five minutes here and fifteen minutes there—time, time, time —it haunts us all.

Isn't it strange, after that, to remember that time has no real existence; that it is only a category of human thought; that there are no calendars, for instance, in heaven; that eternity is not time drawn-out but timelessness. We humans are obliged to think of time because we have an awareness of successiveness, and to tidy up the experience of successiveness we think in the category of time.

But it is all a convention really.

And it is all the more strange that this should be, in a sense, a convention, when we remember that a false handling of time tricks many of us for more than half a lifetime into wishing life away. We grasp at it, yet we fritter it. We want to live, and yet we tend to sponge life out.

You remember, when we were children, how time dragged. We were always wishing the days away to our birthday, or to some party, or to Christmas, or to the holidays. We were always wanting to grow up. If, when we were ten, somebody guessed us as twelve, we were quite proud. We would refer to some poor, unfortunate child six months younger than ourselves as 'that kid'. And nothing that our parents could say to us could prevent us wishing time foolishly away.

Many people are still wishing life away in their teens. They fall in love, perhaps, and a few years pass before they can marry. They wish it away. They haven't the patience to say: 'Let us enjoy what we have now.' They just long for the years to pass when they will have a nest of their own. And then the children come, and they start wishing for the time when the children will be grown up, or when the children go to school. And if things are a little bit difficult economically, they start wishing for the children to be out at work and earning, and by this time they are getting middle-aged, and grey, and bald, and then father starts looking forward to the time when he will retire.

The folly of it. If only somebody could teach us quite young to live in the 'now'. Many, many people are old before they learn that great and precious lesson of life. It is when they can see very little else of life left, and when some of them realize that they have precious little faith in any after-life, that it begins to dawn on their silly minds that they have been wishing the gift away.

I believe God gives a glory to every period of life. I believe that the people who are wise—the people who live with Him —learn how to take the glory from each succeeding age. If you ask those people—those who have really learned the secret—at any stage of their life, 'What is the most glorious period of life?' they will always say: 'Now! Now!'

And they are not foolish; they are wise.

There are some senses in which God's time is always 'now'.

'Today if you will hear His voice.' 'Now is the acceptable time.'

Let me, on this last Sabbath Day of the year, try to impress three simple truths about time on your minds—and on my own as well.

First, *the past is not dead.*

Many of our ideas of time are mistaken. We think that time past is dead. Omar Khayyám thought so. He called for another drink with that in mind.

Ah, fill the Cup:—what boots it to repeat
How Time is slipping underneath our Feet:
Unborn Tomorrow, and dead Yesterday,
Why fret about them if Today is sweet!

'Dead Yesterday'?

Yesterday is not dead; it is alive, vibrant, fecund, making today and shaping tomorrow.

Look at this drunken sot. O no! he is not drunk at the moment. That is because he's spent up, but give him a pound and he'll manage it. Look at him—with no other thought in his fuddled mind than where the next drink is coming from.

He was a gentleman once. You can catch it at times in the intonation of his voice. There is a quaint, old-world courtesy about him in his intervals of soberness; all he has salvaged from the days of his decency.

Sixteen years he has been like this. Would you say that those sixteen years were dead? Would to God they were! They are alive; they are *in* him; it is those sixteen years that make him what he is.

But look also at this old saint of God. What a face! How beautiful it is! I hardly realized that a man could have a *beautiful* face. But how else will you describe that serenity of old age? No youth—however handsome he might be—could have a face like this. This is distilled goodness; this is mature, and mellow, and ripened, and when the old man smiles it is like the light being turned on in a dark room. How did he get such a face? Ah! from his yesterdays. They are all alive in his character, and his character is mirrored in his face. He is one slow to understand mischief and ever swift to do good. Here is the essence of a thousand hours of secret prayer and of a heart ever open to the God of purity and holy love. All his yesterdays are here, alive, and gloriously compelling.

Yesterday is not dead. That is the first mistake we must correct. Time past is not dead time.

II

Here is the second thing I would stress: *The future is not ours.*

People are fond of saying, especially to the young: 'You have the future.'

Well—can you be sure of it?

I hope you have, but—in the language of the book-maker—could you call it a 'cert'?

There are few mistakes more common and more tragic than to count on the future. Cecil Rhodes planned big things: big things for his own future, and big things for Africa also, and died at forty-nine saying: 'So little done; so much to do.'

Keats died at twenty-five; Shelley at thirty; Byron at thirty-six. Friends had prophesied a great future for each of them, but none of them really reached middle-age.

You cannot count with absolute confidence on to-morrow.

I had a sad letter last week from a girl about the death of her father.

'He was so full of plans for the future', she said. 'But he suddenly collapsed on Thursday morning and died before we could get him to the hospital.'

We are all mortal. There is no ground for morbidity in this; it is just plain horse-sense to look at the conditions on which we hold life here.

When you take a job you accept certain conditions of contract; a month's notice either way, or a week's. There is no such contract when you accept life. A moment's notice is all you may receive.

A few years ago, in a restaurant not half a mile from here, at the annual dinner of a certain association opposed to religion, their chairman for the year was making an after-dinner speech. The orchestra were tuning their instruments in the next room. The chairman was lampooning religion and guffawing over the vision the apostle Paul saw on the Damascus road. Presently—all the papers reported it the next morning—in the middle of a blasphemous sentence, he just went pale and sat down. He was dead. 'Heart failure', said the coroner.

The notice can be as short as that.

The future is not ours.

III

Here is the third thing: *Now is the acceptable time*.

The only time we have is *now*. It is literally true to say that 'now is the acceptable time' in the sense that it is the only time you can possibly accept. It is in the very nature of time to come to you moment by moment.

Somebody tried once to scare Will Rogers, the cowboy philosopher, by asking him: 'If you had only forty-eight hours to live how would you spend them?'

Will Rogers replied: 'One at a time.'

You can only accept time as it comes. Therefore, in *that* sense, now is the acceptable time. It is the present you have. How are you spending time now? What could happen before this service comes to a close?

(1) Listen! *God's forgiveness is now*. Now! Isn't that a wonderful announcement to make? Years of sin—forgiven in a moment! Is it possible? Is that a credible statement? Does that make sense in a moral universe?

C

I do not know whether that makes sense in your idea of a moral universe, but I say that is the gospel. God's forgiveness is *now*. For Jesus Christ's sake, He meets penitence with pardon, and He meets it *now*.

> *In wonder lost, with trembling joy*
> *We take the pardon of our God;*
> *Pardon for crimes of deepest dye,*
> *A pardon bought with Jesu's blood:*
> *Who is a pardoning God like Thee?*
> *Or who has grace so rich and free?"*

Listen to the Parable of the Prodigal Son as Jesus *didn't* tell it:

And he arose and set out for his home, and when at last he arrived at the door, he banged and there was no response. He stood there in his piteous rags and hunger for a while, and then he knocked again and a third time; and finally a window opened and his father looked out and said: 'O! it's you. You're spent up, I suppose. You look a nice beauty. What have you come home for? You've had your share of everything. You know where to come when you're hungry . . .'

And he said: 'Father, I have sinned against Heaven and in thy sight . . .', but his father banged the window and left him for a while on the doorstep. Presently, his father opened the door and said: 'You're an utter disgrace to me and to all your relatives. I'm ashamed of you; utterly ashamed. But I'm your father, and I've thought it out, and I am prepared to put you on probation for three months, and if, at the end of three months I can find no fault in you, well, perhaps I'll have it in my heart to give you another start. . . .'

That is the Parable of the Prodigal Son as Jesus *didn't* tell it. As you hear me say it, your heart cries out against its falsity. 'Lies!' you say. 'Lies!' And you are right; they *are* lies.

'And while he was yet a long way off his father saw him, and had compassion, and ran and fell on his neck and kissed him.' (No probationary period, you notice. No talk of three months. No, it was instant. It was now! Now!) 'The robe', he cries. 'The ring, the ring, the robe, the robe.'

'Now is the acceptable time. *Today* if you will hear my voice.'

The trouble is that when God says 'Today' we so often say 'Tomorrow'. 'Yes, tomorrow; *for certain*, tomorrow. Tomorrow I will begin the new life. Tomorrow I will walk with God.'

And when the morrow comes, you are still saying: 'Tomorrow.'

And so the years pass. Will death come and still find you saying, 'Tomorrow'; 'tomorrow'?

Don't say 'Tomorrow'. '*Today*, if you will hear His voice.'

(2) Here is another precious thing. God says '*Now*' *for the gift of the Holy Spirit*—for cleansing and for power.

One of the favourite words with John Wesley and Charles Wesley, and all the leaders of the Evangelical Revival, was the word 'Now'.

It always *is* with true evangelical preaching: 'Now.'

When Wesley spoke about a birth in holiness happening in a moment, he shocked many of the religious people of the eighteenth century, and they said: 'But it is absurd. You cannot be holy in a moment. It is a slow growth. This is dangerous blasphemy, in such a connection, to talk of "now".'

But still they went on saying it. Charles Wesley sang:

> *Saviour, to Thee my soul looks up,*
> *My present Saviour Thou!*
> *In all the confidence of hope,*
> *I claim the blessing now.*

People said: 'All growth is gradual, not sudden. It cannot be sudden.'

And John Wesley said: 'How is it with birth? There is a growth in the womb before birth and there is a long growth after birth, but birth itself is sudden. When that strange, mysterious downward thrust forces the child into life . . . it is sudden. You can mark it on the calendar and time it on the clock.'

Said Wesley: 'It is like that in the things of the Spirit. There is a maturing before the moment, and there can be long development after the moment, but the moment itself is a moment—and that moment can be now.'

Even now, at your earnest desiring, the Holy Spirit could enter your heart to cleanse it from evil, to break the power of cancelled sin, to give you freedom where before you were in bondage, and victory where before you were in defeat. 'Today if you will hear His voice.' Now!

We all of us know people in whose company it seems easy to be good; who have the breath of God about them; who speak—even when they are not speaking—of holy things; who unconsciously lift us Heaven-ward.

Sometimes we think, in our stumbling efforts to be good, 'how easy virtue would be if we were always in the company of these choice souls. Fancy being Timothy to Paul, or Mark to Peter, or Leo to Saint Francis, or Wesley to John Fletcher, or Railton to William Booth. Fancy living near to such radiant souls and drinking in their goodness; to have that sublime example always at hand. How our poor lives would flower in the warmth of their atmosphere.'

Yet all those yearnings are, in a sense, mistaken.

God has promised not merely to live with us, but *in* us. God, the Holy Spirit, will come and dwell in any heart now. Anyone who truly desires Him, and will fulfil the conditions, may receive Him, and He will take up His residence now.

'*Today*, if you will hear His voice.'

What a glad farewell to the old year! What a gay fearlessness concerning all that the future may have in store!

I am not saying 'Later on'—that phrase you so hated in your childhood. This is the word of the Saviour to you: '*Now!*' '*Today* if you will hear My voice.'

4

He Makes All Things New

Ecclesiastes 1⁹—*There is no new thing under the sun*
Revelation 21⁵—*Behold, I make all things new*

THE BOOK of Ecclesiastes is deeply pessimistic in
tone; it has been called a 'Treatise on the Illusion
of Life'. The word 'vanity' (which might be better
translated 'nothingness') occurs forty times and is the
key-note of the whole book. ' "Vanity of vanities", says
the Preacher. "All is vanity." "Nothing of nothingness",
says the Preacher. "All is nothing." '

The book begins by describing existence as a meaningless and barren cycle of events which goes on occurring
again and again in endless repetition. Nature and mankind are compelled to perform a dreary chain of deeds
which only repeats all that has gone before. The sun goes
on rising and setting. The wind blows north to south, and
then south to north. The rivers run into the sea—and
never fill it. Men look, 'but the eye is not satisfied with
seeing'. They listen, but 'the ear is not filled with hearing'.
What has been, shall be. Men think they find something
new, but that is illusion. It has already existed in the ages
gone by. 'There is no new thing under the sun.'

The theory that all life is just one endless repetition has
often been put forward in the history of thought and
notably in the most spacious days of Greece. The ruling
word of the great Greek thinkers was not the word
'progress' (as with our forebears in the nineteenth
century), but the word 'cycle'. Vastly improbable as

it may seem to us, there are certain things still worthy of serious attention, which lend plausibility to the view that all history repeats itself. Excavations in Egypt, Asia and Mexico give us glimpses of ancient civilizations not unworthy of comparison with our own. Sir Flinders Petrie, the distinguished Egyptologist, once asserted that civilization is a recurring phenomenon on the earth. The men of old time knew some things that the craftsmen and artists of our own day have not found out. They knew how to harden copper, for instance, by a process which we clever people haven't rediscovered yet. The Greek standard of beauty in sculpture outsoars our highest modern achievements. In some ways we have not surpassed the Romans in our knowledge of the principles of law. We may boast our steamships, wireless, cinemas and television, and feel certain that these were unknown among men before our era, but while we have gained in some ways we may have lost in others. It would be untrue to assert that all life is mere repetition, but a great deal of history has a way of repeating itself and nobody is likely to deny that there is a certain sameness about our individual lives; a dull monotony, a lack of freshness, a prosy, flat, commonplace-ness that becomes at times almost unbearable.

Whether or not the Greeks were right about their 'cycles' or the moderns right about their 'progress', no one can deny this, that our own life repeats itself; that one week is remarkably like the week before, and that in its broad outline each year is very similar to the last. This new year is not likely to be an exception to the rule.

Eat! Work! Sleep! The same old routine over and over again. We can only have life on the terms on which it is offered and sometimes we think they are not very good terms. In days of extra depression or satiety, we are inclined to say with the author of Ecclesiastes: 'There is no new thing under the sun.'

I

But let us look at the second text. 'He that sitteth on the Throne said, Behold, I make all things new.' It is taken from John's great vision of the Holy City. In its apocalyptic sense I do not use it today. I want to take this great word and set it in the context of your life now. I want to apply it to those of you who are finding life wearisome and monotonous. God says: 'Behold, I make all things new.'

All things new? This would be great news if it were true. Can He take the monotony away from life? Can He make it fresh and bright and thrilling?

Yes. He can do all that. He can give you a new world, with new delights and new comforts, and new hopes and new ends. No! not by changing your external world, but changing *you*.

I know what you are saying in your heart if you have followed me until now. 'How does He do that?'

Let me put a question to you. How would you expect Him to do it? Suppose I were to ask you what you would require to have the really happy new year which other people have been wishing you so freely of late; what conditions would you lay down for the achievement of that happiness?

I fancy I know the line on which your wishes would run. Some of you would say: 'If I had an extra pound a week I would be happy.' Others would insist that they need another house, away from the tiresome neighbours—or any kind of house so long as you could have it to yourselves. Some of you would ask for a better job or shorter hours. You would heap together your varied circumstances and you would say, in effect, that, if only *this* were changed, or *that*, undoubtedly you would be happy.

My friends, I cannot offer you any one of these things. In some instances, I wish I could. If it were in my power

I would enlarge the income of some of you and seek a
better environment for others, but I want to insist that
those are not the major things and if I could not point you
to something else I do not think that, in giving you those
things only, I would be giving you enough.

The major question which lies behind all these debatings
is just this: 'Does your happiness reside in your circumstances or in yourselves?' Important as circumstances are,
I insist that the fount of happiness must be from God in
ourselves. As my ministry lengthens and widens, I can
look back and remember being intimate with men and
women in the most varied circumstances, and I say
plainly that an adequate income, and a pleasant house,
and kindly neighbours, and a decent job, cannot of themselves produce happiness. I have known men who pos-
sessed them all, and yet were miserable.

I had a man in one of my churches, a wealthy man, who
suffered heavy reverses when the cotton slump came, but
who admitted to me that, despite this loss, his income still
stood at £30 a week. (That was much more then than
now!) He was not a happy man. I have sometimes
quoted the instance of Edward Fitzgerald, the translator of
The Rubà'iyàt of Omar Khayyám, a man to whom our
Christian Faith seemed to make only the slightest appeal
and who was quite sure that he could get a happy life
if only he could mould his circumstances in the right way.
So he took a little place in the country and he parted
from his wife (with whom he did not agree), and he kept
doves as the most congenial hobby for a man seeking
peace, and he used his mind and money to mould precisely the circumstances which would produce happiness,
but, in the end, he seems to have missed it.

And, in contrast to both these instances, let me say
that I have known people whose whole income was
beneath the notice of a serious financier, who lived in a wee

back room, and who had never known all their lives what it was to have a real financial margin, but who had the joy of God in their hearts and His song on their lips.

Don't think I despise circumstances. You would do me an injustice. But we are dealing with things primary and I say that happiness does not reside in circumstances; it resides in you. When people have wished you a happy new year the question it should have raised in your mind should not have concerned the externals of your life but the condition of your spiritual health and the degree of your intimacy with God.

I cannot promise you, in the coming year, a new set of circumstances. Indeed, I anticipate, for myself and for you, difficulties and disappointments and obstacles and some pain—for that is life. No year has yet dawned which did not contain them and, if such a year did come, it might be debilitating to the soul. But, in the name of Him who sits upon the Throne, I promise you that if you will receive Him into your heart, and if you will submit to His Lordship over you, you can have a new heart, a new life, and, therefore, a new birth.

I cannot beckon you away from the flinty path on which some of you walk. I am not commissioned to do so. Those who follow Christ must travel at times 'by stony paths and rugged ways'. But I do promise you, even in grey times, new life in God.

Paul said: 'If any man is in Christ, he is a new creature; the old things are passed away; behold they are become new.'

Billy Bray declared on the day of his conversion; 'I remember this, that everything looked new to me, the fields, the cattle, the trees. I was like a new man in a new world.'

Temple Gairdner went from Trinity College, Oxford, the morning after his surrender to Christ and ordered an illuminated text for his wall: 'Behold, I make all things new.'

II

(1) Let me illustrate what I mean when I say that *a change in oneself can mean a change in the whole scene*. Let me take the simplest illustration.

I was once asked, when I was a minister in the North, if I would find time to cheer up a young man who had been sent to our neighbourhood to recuperate after a nervous breakdown. I promised to do my best. I sought the young man out and I began but, O, it was hard work. 'This is a grey world,' he said. 'I see no purpose in it. It is dull, meaningless and evil. Its pleasures soon pass. Its pains endure. I seriously ask myself the question: "Is life worth having?"'—and much more—*very much more*—in the same strain.

I saw him once or twice a week for nearly two months, and every conversation was the same—and then something happened to that young man! He fell in love. None of this nervous, hesitant venturing into the waters. He took a header! And on the day his engagement was announced (and it followed very soon) he came and saw me and began the conversation with words something like this: 'This is a lovely world. Come out into the garden and listen to that little bird singing fit to burst its heart. Isn't it a glorious morning? How good it is to be alive.'

I listened to his raptures in reverent silence and all my smiles were up my sleeve. It was just the same old world he had been castigating for months. Just the same; no better and no worse. The change was all in him. I rounded off the little episode by marrying them, and I pass the parable on to you. There are people here who find life horribly dull, commonplace and matter of fact, but if they fell in love with Jesus Christ, what a difference it would make. All things would become

new. They would walk down familiar paths but they
would see unfamiliar things. The scent of wayside flowers,
the courage of common people, the lovely loyalty of the
hard-pressed—and opportunity in every day to show
forth the love of their new-found Lord. Old friends, old
scenes will lovelier be—if only they would begin this
new year with a supreme act of confession and consecration to Him. I believe that if I had all the wisdom of
the ages, I could give you no better advice than this.
I believe if I had all the heaped-up treasures of fabled
plutocrats, I could give you nothing equal in value to
an introduction to Christ. Covenant yourselves, therefore,
with the covenant-keeping God. He dispels monotony.
He makes all things new.

(2) Here is the second thing I want to stress. *A changed
man, by God's grace, often changes his own circumstances.*
Character moulds circumstances and environment, as
well as environment and circumstances moulding character. You have heard, I imagine, the oft-told story of the man
who expressed the strong opinion that the most beautiful
word in the English language was the word 'which'. When
his friends dissented from his odd idea, he said this:

'I was once a drunken sot. All my money went into
the pub. Every Saturday, I soaked until I was nearly
spent up, and then I rolled home and flung the few
remaining shillings in my wife's lap. With a spate of
obscene language I told her to stop her snivelling and to
be thankful for what she had got. Through all the years
I was a slave to drink, I never had a smart rag to my back.
I hated myself and most decent people despised me.
Then I met God and was gloriously changed. I listened
to a preacher's message, responded to his appeal, and a
wonderful power came into my life and revolutionized
me. I cut the drink out entirely. I dropped my filthy

talk and gave my wife her proper week's money and began to buy little extras for the home. As the months went by, I gathered a wardrobe.

'One summer evening, six months after I was converted, I said to my wife: "Let us go out for a walk", and she went upstairs to put her hat and coat on. While she was upstairs I called out, "Bring my overcoat down with you", and she said "Which?" Which! I could not answer for the moment. I was staggered by the word "which". I had *two*.' The poor, odorous rag-bag who had been a pillar of the pubs had two overcoats.

Do you see the point? He was changed, and, by God's grace, circumstances changed with him. Your circumstances may be capable of some change even as circumstances. The very mould of your life, and of which you complain so bitterly, may be capable of transformation, if you are transformed yourself. There are awful frustrations in life, and sometimes we can only endure them. But the greatest frustration is the sin inside us and when that is dealt with, it sometimes happens that the external frustrations frustrate us no more.

You have not forgotten, I suppose, the workman who was chaffed by his workmates because he lived a life of strict sobriety, never gambled, and always spoke of the Bible with reverence.

'If you believe in the Bible', they said, 'you must believe that water was turned into wine.'

'I believe more than that', he said. His mind went back to his evil early days and his pre-conversion years.

'I have seen', he said, 'beer turned into furniture. Betting-slips turned into food. I have seen a woman, miserable because she was married to a gambling addict, made radiantly and permanently happy because her man was changed before her eyes. Of course I believe in miracles.'

A changed man changes his environment.

(3) Here is the third thing I would mention (though I cannot fully develop it): *The change Christ can make extends beyond individuals to families, communities, businesses—and could extend to nations and the whole world.*

Some of you will think I am ignoring the ugly facts of sin in this life.

Some will say that I am ignoring that we 'wrestle . . . against principalities, against powers, against rulers of the darkness of this world, against spiritual wickedness in high places'.

Some will remind me of the apocalyptic aspect of this promise (which we agreed to leave aside as we began) and insist that this promise belongs to ages and to an order beyond our present observation.

I still ask you to remember the power of our Lord to change society as well as persons. He can make *all* things new. We have to work with Him not only for the salvation of individuals, but for the Christianizing of the social order too.

Think of Kidderminster when Richard Baxter was minister there. Not a house without family prayer! Divine love seeming to fill the place!

Hold His power of transformation in your reverent imagination for a moment. Think what he could do for you, your home, your business, your town.

Go forward into the New Year with courage. His transformation begins inside us and there isn't one of us—however mature we are in the faith—in whom He could not work *some* change.

Ask Him to do it. Let us pray together in the silence for that very thing.

5

His Destination is in His Face

*Luke 9*⁵³—*And they did not receive him, because his face was as though he were going to Jerusalem*

JESUS CHRIST found the world an inhospitable place. At His birth, it provided no warmer welcome than a cattle-shed, and His life of loving service was cut short by His brutal murder at thirty-three.

He wasn't wanted.

Nor is the inhospitality of the world seen only at His birth and death. All through His life He was receiving proof of it. He came, on one occasion, Matthew tells us, to the country of the Gadarenes, and they besought Him to 'depart from their borders'.

He came, on another occasion, to Nazareth, His own native place, and, because they disapproved a sermon He preached in their synagogue, they took Him to the brow of a hill and had a mind to assassinate Him.

And (on this occasion to which my text refers), tired at the end of a journey, and in great stress of soul, He came to a Samaritan village to ask accommodation for the night, and they, with one accord, shut their doors in His face.

It wouldn't have been so bad if He had been a cold and self-contained man, indifferent to human sympathies and intent only on His task.

But He was warm with love. He came giving and seeking affection; He was sensitive to rebuff and, every time the inhospitality of the world was shown to Him, a wounded heart beat within His breast.

I want us, as we enter Lent, to look at this incident a little more closely.

I

Jesus, the Scripture tells us, was on His way to Jerusalem. It was His last visit to the capital. Therefore, He was on His way to die. The shadow of the Cross was already upon Him. The evangelists stress His high purposiveness in this hour. Luke says: 'He stedfastly set His face to go to Jerusalem.' He measured Himself to what was ahead.

The Cross was not just a trap cunningly contrived which startled Him by its unexpectedness. He saw the trap. He walked into it. He foresaw, and He foresaw in this hour, what would await Him in Jerusalem. When the hour came, in no doubt of His Father's will, He willingly stretched Himself on the wood.

And, as day after day of the journey to the capital passed, it was His custom to send a couple of disciples ahead of the main body and say to them: 'Make some arrangements in a village for our hospitality for the night.'

On this occasion, they came to a village of the Samaritans and sought accommodation there.

Now, most people who study the Scriptures know that there was enmity between the Jews and the Samaritans, but not everybody knows why the enmity existed. It had, as many of these racial enmities have, its roots in history.

It went back to the year 722 B.C. when Sargon, the king of Assyria, sacked Samaria and carried away the Ten Tribes into captivity.

But, as you can well believe, these wholesale deportations of ancient times were never absolutely complete, but always, when a people had been carried away, a remnant of the population was left upon the soil.

And so it was in Samaria; and when Sargon, the king

of Assyria, sowed that devasted area with his Assyrian settlers, they found a remnant of the Israelites still in occupation of the land. In course of time, the Israelites and the Assyrians inter-married and made one people, who were called 'Samaritans'.

Now, you begin to see why the Jews and the Samaritans were at daggers drawn.

The Jews said: 'They are not of the pure stock of Israel.' Nor did the Samaritans improve their position in the eyes of the Jews when they developed a religion which was closely akin to Judaism. They took the Pentateuch and said, 'This is our Holy Book as well'; and, because they were excluded from Mount Zion (from Jerusalem), they said, 'We will have a holy mount of our own', and they fixed it at Mount Gerizim in Samaria. Both national and religious sentiment nourished in the Jew a whole-souled and bitter contempt for his cousin of Samaria. It was not unlike the feeling which the pure-bred Greek entertained for the Macedonian.

Jewish legislation bore many marks of this hatred. If a Samaritan, for any reason at all, wanted to offer a sacrifice in the temple at Jerusalem, he had to come in on the same level as a slave or a heathen.

If a Samaritan witnessed a Jewish bill of divorcement, that simple fact alone invalidated the bill.

Among the Jews, the word 'Samaritan' was about the nastiest term you could use. It meant 'dog'. It meant 'devil'. It meant 'illegitimate'.

Among the Samaritans the term 'Jew' meant 'snob', 'stiff-necked', 'haughty'.

When Jesus asked (you remember) the Samaritan woman at Jacob's well for a drink, she was astonished. She said: 'How is it that Thou, being a Jew, asketh drink of me, which am a woman of Samaria? For the Jews have no dealings with the Samaritans.'

D

If you had called a Jew, in the time of Jesus, a 'Samaritan', it would have been the dirtiest insult you could have thought of; it would have been a deliberate and calculated aspersion of the foulest kind.

But if you were to call *me* a 'Samaritan' today, it would be one of the highest compliments you could pay me! I should be flattered. You would mean that I was full of the milk of human kindness and bursting with practical zeal.

What has happened to the world? It has been completely changed.

Who changed it?

Jesus changed it.

He told a story. He tossed it off one day—like that (!) —in the midst of His preaching: a simple story about a robber-infested road, a bleeding victim, a callous priest and Levite, a despised Samaritan, a wondering innkeeper, a receipted bill.

Jesus told it—but it picked that word out of the gutter and washed it clean. It took that term from the vocabulary of the brothel and made it adjectival of the saints. Jesus did it—this same Jesus, who, at the end of His tired day, and in great stress of soul, came to this Samaritan village and said: 'May I come in?'

And they all, with one accord, shut their doors in His face.

My friends, here is a mystery! Let us clear up this mystery if we can!

Why did they all, with such unanimity, turn away our blessed Lord? Why?

Because He was Jesus? No, not because of that. I give them credit for seeing that His face (even on this distressing journey) was 'full of grace and truth'. No! not because He was Jesus.

'O!' you say, 'I know. Of course—because He was a Jew.'

No! not even because of that.

They were flattered more than they were embittered by that. They must have said to themselves: 'Aren't we getting on now? The Jews want to stay with us.'

No, not because He was a Jew.

The Scriptures give it to us in the phrase I am expounding now: 'They did not receive Him, because His face was as though He were going to Jerusalem.'

Strange phrase! Did He carry His destination on His face? 'Because His face was as though He were going to Jerusalem'?

They knew where He was going. He was on His way to Zion.

> *He was marching to Zion;*
> *Beautiful, beautiful Zion,*
> *He was marching upward to Zion,*
> *The beautiful City of God.*

And they knew He was staying only a night.

They were saying this, in effect, if I understand their mind aright: 'We don't mind you being a Jew. We want to get rid of this old trouble between our peoples. Stay with us. Make your abode here. Worship on our holy mount. Be one with us and we'll have you.

'But if, tomorrow morning, you are going to arise and display that heart yearning for Zion; if, at the dawn, you are going to take that steep ascent to Jerusalem— we *don't* want you. You disturb us with a sense of our inferiority. There is no room for you here.'

I am sure that that was it, and I am sure, now that I see the inwardness of it, why it can mean so much to you and me today.

All through His earthly life, and all through His ministry in this world since, Jesus Christ has come to men and women where they are; just where they are.

But never will He stay where they are. Never! He says: 'Come with Me. I'm marching to Zion. Come with Me—to the heights!'

But men and women have not reacted in that way. They have tried to keep Him at their own level—and He won't be kept.

Let us look at that a little more closely.

II

I say that Jesus Christ comes to men and women just where they are. There are not many people of whom that can be said.

If you, knowing nothing about music, were to go to a professor of music for lessons, the probability is that he would say: 'Well—get through the earlier stages with someone else. Let somebody else teach you the five-finger exercises. Come to me later.'

Not so with Jesus! He comes to men and women where they are. He comes to Simon, a blaspheming fisherman at his nets. He comes to Matthew, a traitorous and extortionate tax-collector, at his desk. He came to Bunyan, the wandering tinker, and He came to John Wesley, an Oxford graduate and a don. He comes to men just where they are. Not ignorance, nor learning; not fancied superiorities nor inferiorities, can keep Him out. He comes to men and women just where they are. But He will not stay where they are!

He's marching to Zion. He wants men and women to march with Him. He has plans. He can change their lives; He can change society; He can change the world. He wants them to march with Him.

So many of them won't march with Him. They like Him, but they don't like the things that He is out for. They would keep Him at their level, and they will not travel where He goes.

And that is why I say that this experience in this Samaritan village was no unusual experience for our Lord. It has been His experience a million million times since.

He comes to a man who is living for money—and how many there are! You can live for money without having much of it. You live for it when you think it is the only thing worth living for. He comes to a man living for money, and He says: 'May I come in?' And the man says: 'Welcome, Lord—if you are content with things at my level.'

And then the luminous eyes of Jesus search his soul, and he sees at a glance what Jesus will do with him and his money. He will give him a sense of stewardship. He will teach him dispersal, tithing, large generosity.

The man fears—and shuts the door in His face. He will not receive Him, because 'His face is as though He would go to Jerusalem'.

Some years ago I went to Pompeii and saw that city so strangely hidden in the dust and ashes of the centuries. I went to the very edge of the new excavations and watched the tragedy as though it had happened only the year before.

I saw at Pompeii, not far from one of the gateways, the skeleton of a man who, to all appearances, had not fled when the volcano gave its first warnings but had run back for his trinkets. And there is his skeleton now —and the trinkets! They are gold, but they looked strangely green and mouldy lying at his side.

He ran back for the bangles and he lost his life.

O! the folly of it; that people should put such surpassing value on the treasures of this earth and not see that the only treasure laid up where moth and rust do not corrupt are the treasures laid up in heaven; the things which time cannot tarnish; which will shine in time and in eternity, too.

Or Jesus comes to some younger man who is out for a

good time. He hasn't defined, maybe, very closely what he means by 'having a good time', but his own pleasure is clearly in view.

And Jesus arrests him with the words: 'Any room for Me?'

The young man has heard about Jesus; strange things, maybe; that Jesus believes the sweetest joys are born of the deepest consecration; that Jesus is One who would have us serving others; who demands a maximum from all who take His commission; who will wander into every dirty recess of one's heart and clean it out; and examine every shabby motive and make it pure.

The young man is fearful. The price is too high. He shuts the door in His face. He will not receive Him because 'His face is as though He would go to Jerusalem'.

I have never found it hard to get a cheer for Jesus Christ in the open air or, at least, a warm sense of approval. O no! People will stand around, and, when you say a good word for Jesus Christ, they say a good word too—and some Christian people think that's wonderful and proves that England is a Christian land.

Does it?

Men at a football match will take their hats off and sing 'Abide with me', and some Christian people think that's wonderful also—and the prelude to revival.

O! my friends, it isn't a cheer we want for Jesus. It wasn't a cheer He asked for Himself. He said: 'If any man would come after Me, let him deny himself and take up his cross and follow Me.'

You see? It isn't a cheer; it's discipleship. It isn't admiration; it's consecration. Will you march with Him to Zion? Will you go on with Him to the Cross?

III

So we enter Lent!

For many centuries, this season of our Church year has been a season of spiritual discipleship and solemn preparation for Calvary. Let it be that for all of us again. If a weekly fast—or some other form of self-denial helps you—keep it. But have one object in mind; to go step by step with your Saviour to the Cross. Put yourself imaginatively in the place of those Samaritans—and then reverse their behaviour! Welcome Him to your home and heart. Do even more! Rise tomorrow morning resolved to go with Him to Jerusalem. On every day in Lent give some time to meditating on the purposes of God on earth and your relationship to them. You cannot fail to come to Good Friday challenged, humbled, mortified and (I trust) redeemed and re-made.

We need this annual 'Check-up' to our spiritual lives. Even those of us no longer young in discipleship know how easy it is to slip back. The sheer inertia of our nature, as well as the unsubdued sin in our souls, tends all the time to make us drag our feet. Lent is here to brace us to our journey again. We can come once more to Calvary totally re-committed to our Lord and invulnerable in Him.

Let me help you in this self-examination—and help myself as well—by putting to you a few personal questions which we could all consider as we walk with Christ to the Cross.

Am I clean in thought, word, and deed?

Is Christ (so far as I can make Him) the Head of my home?

Do they know I am a Christian where I work?

Are other people likely to be drawn to better things for knowing me?

Do I guard time each day for prayer and my Bible?

Do I go regularly to Church and to the holy table?

Do other people find it easy to work with me in Christian work?

Am I generous (so far as I am honestly able) to good causes?

Am I growing in Christ?

Dwell especially on this last question. How many years have you been a professing Christian? Has it been steady growth or were you keener, more effective, more ardent once than you are now?

You can't really stay motionless in the Christian life. It is growth or decay.

Which will you choose?

I don't know much about natural history but friends of mine who do, tell me that there is a species of crab which periodically sheds its shell. At one time the shell is its home, its refuge, its all—but if it does not shed its shell at the time it should, that same shell becomes its prison and finally its tomb.

How is it with you?

Did you set out boldly in the Christian life, but now flag on the way? Is it no longer an uttermost consecration? —no more a maximum for God? Are there reservations in your dedication?—and 'ifs' and parentheses in your prayers?

Well—Lent is here. Let us use the season for the closer companionship of our Blessed Lord and, in the divine company, recover the lost lustre of our soiled souls.

6

He is Lonelier than the Loneliest

John 16³²—*Behold, the hour cometh, yea, is now come,
that ye shall be scattered, every man to his own, and shall
leave me alone*

IT IS HARD to the point of impossibility for mortals to
understand all the sufferings of the Saviour, but I want
to dwell today on one ingredient of the bitter cup. I
want to dwell on the awful loneliness of Jesus Christ.
'Behold, the hour cometh, yea, is now come, that ye shall
be scattered, every man to his own, and shall leave me
alone.'

I

When the Gospel narrative opens, we seldom see Jesus
except in a crowd. 'The people thronged Him', we read.
'The multitude followed Him.' 'They could not get near
Him because of the crowd.' Always—except, of course,
when He drew aside for secret prayer—He seems to be in
the midst of a crowd.

But, if you turn swiftly to the end from the beginning,
what a change! The awful, awful loneliness of Calvary!

Most people have had some experience of loneliness. I
do not doubt that there are lonely people in reach of my
voice now, but it goes beyond question that there was
never loneliness like His.

In a sense He was lonely even when the crowds were
thronging Him. Companionship is not communion. I
shared many a meal with men in the Army with whom I
could never share a thought. All sensible people know

that one can be lonely in a crowd. When you think of loneliness, don't think of the wide, open, and empty spaces; think of a railway station with someone meeting every other passenger—but you. You will feel lonely then.

Or think of a great vessel about to sail across the Atlantic and every passenger with someone to see them off— but you.

When I was ordained to the ministry in the city of York, many other men were ordained at the same time. All had their relatives and friends present but I. When I stood up after that solemn service and looked about me, every man the centre of a group of delighted friends, I had never felt so lonely before.

But could the Son of God be other than lonely—with a loneliness more awful than we can conceive?

Human greatness is lonely. When the Prince Consort died, Tennyson wrote of the 'lonely splendour' in which his death had left the Crown; and Queen Victoria herself has told how, in one of her last interviews with him, the aged poet said to her: 'You are so alone on that terrible height; it is terrible.' And if humans can be lonely among humans, how unspeakably lonely must the incarnate Son of God have been.

Now, the nearer our Lord got to the Cross, the lonelier He became. Thousands of the people who followed Him didn't care a jot for the things that meant so much to Him. Some were seeking signs and wonders; some were eager to hear how He would answer His critics; some thought He had come to found an earthly kingdom and they left Him the moment they concluded that He hadn't. The Scriptures say plainly: 'Upon this many of his disciples went back, and walked no more with him.'

Many men who are misunderstood in the world find solace in their own homes and with their family. Principal Rainey, the distinguished Scottish ecclesiastic, who had some terrible disappointments to bear in life, was once asked how he could go on in the face of them all, and he answered: 'O! you see, I am so happy at home.'

Gladstone had his sad moments in the conduct of affairs, and there were times when—not adulation—but wide and bitter criticism was his portion.

If you were to ask how he bore it, the simple answer is this; he was so happy at home.

When all the world takes arms against you, it is grand to feel that there are a few folk at home who will take arms beside you against all the world.

But Jesus had not that consolation. His family—even His dear mother—failed to understand Him. His words and His deeds had made Him a public figure, and some of the bitter rancour raised by His teaching reacted on them. The family found themselves marked out, and talked about, until they were plagued by it. His brothers and sisters came home many times, I imagine, and said to their mother: 'Everybody's talking about Jesus again, Mother. They say he insulted the learned scribes to their face. Some of the Pharisees have come down from Jerusalem. They are very clever men. They say that Jesus is all wrong; indeed, that He is blasphemous. O! it was so lovely when He was at home with us, but He is not Himself; He cannot be.'

And one day they persuaded Mary—Mary who had hid such secret things in her heart—that her dear eldest boy was deranged, and they went off to bring Jesus home.

You know the rest. It is one of the saddest stories in the Gospel history. They came to a house crowded with people listening to Him, and couldn't get near to Him because of the press, so they sent a message in. And you remember His terrible answer. Looking round on the people nearest to Him, and seeing the light of understanding dawn on the face of some of them, He stretched out

His hands and said: 'Behold, my mother and my brethren! For whosoever shall do the will of my Father which is in heaven, he is my brother, and sister—and mother.'

He must have been lonelier than ever after that! The house of Mary and Martha apart—and even there His coming caused domestic tension—there was no place where He was even dimly understood.

Have you ever noticed how Chapter 7 of St John's Gospel ends, and how Chapter 8 begins? It is really one verse. The chapter division comes at the wrong place. 'And they went every man unto his own house: but Jesus went unto the mount of Olives.' Every man had his own house to go to! Everyone—except the Son of God.

II

But it is Passion Sunday and in dealing with the loneliness of our Lord I must needs anticipate the events of Thursday and Friday in Holy Week as well. The increasing loneliness of His way became, in Holy Week, accelerated in its awfulness. In three tremendous experiences of desertion our Lord knew a loneliness no other soul has ever known, or need ever know. Let us glance at them in turn.

(1) First, the people left Him.

From the first days of His ministry He had had a grip upon the people. Many a time He had withstood the rulers because the people were with Him, and many a time the rulers had feared to do Him harm because the people would have risen in revolt.

But when Pilate brought Him to the veranda of the Praetorium, crowned with thorns and robed in a rag, and asked the people themselves, 'What, then, shall I do with Jesus, who is called Christ?'—you know what they said: 'Crucify him; crucify him.'

The *people* said it! Nobody knows how big the crowd was, or how it was composed. It might have been an honest cross-section of the population, or it might have been the ignorant scum of the city, suborned to scream away the life of an innocent man. It was very early in the morning. It is dubious if the ordinary people were about. The whole thing may have been engineered by the priests. The point has been long discussed but no one can tell.

But how could it appear to Jesus? The people—the people—His people—the ones He had come to save—screamed it out together: 'Crucify him; crucify him.'

Don't put too much faith in an ignorant democracy. It was democracy which sentenced Socrates and hounded Haldane out of public life, and crucified the Son of God.

I wonder—as He stood there robed in a rag, crowned in thorns, the blood of the Garden and of the pillar wet upon Him still—I wonder if He said to Himself (as people sometimes do under awful strain): 'What day is it?'

'Friday!'

'Friday?'

'On Sunday they cheered Me and now they curse Me.'

'On Sunday it was "Hosanna" and now it is "Crucify".'

"On Sunday I was their King and now I'm a "criminal".'

'On Sunday all the world went after Me, and now all the world does Me to death.'

The people! The people! He was forsaken by the people.

(2) Notice, in the second place, that He was forsaken by His disciples. They left Him. Yes, it is in the record: 'They all forsook Him, and fled.' Once, it was written, 'They forsook all and followed Him'; but now, 'They all forsook Him and fled'. Peter—though He solemnly warned him; Thomas—though he had said, when they first turned their faces to Jerusalem, 'Let us also go, that we may die with Him'; Andrew—dear, dependable Andrew—even Andrew.

I cannot think that the disciples were just plain cowards.

They were bewildered. Put yourself in their position. They had seen marvels wrought. They had seen the dead raised, the lepers cleansed, the blind receive their sight. They had seen it for nigh three years. How could they know that He would never use His power for Himself? How could they guess that if sin would do this awful thing, love would bear it? He had told them—and not once but many times of late—'The Son of man must suffer'. But they seemed never to take it in, and after Palm Sunday is it surprising that they felt the people would acclaim Him, and He would accept the acclamation?

Yet now, in the shadow of the Cross, they desert Him. He sees them flee. What awful loneliness! Kissed into the arms of His enemies by Judas; denied in the Judgement Hall by Peter; deserted by all. Now, indeed, was the word fulfilled: 'Behold, the hour cometh, yea, is now come, that ye shall be scattered, every man to his own, and shall leave me alone.'

(3) Forsaken by the people; forsaken by the disciples; here is the hardest question of all: Was He forsaken by God?

Listen! Listen to the most awful text in the Bible: 'My God, my God, why hast thou forsaken me?'

Is this, then, the truth? Had He to pass through this awful experience too? Was it to be a loneliness more awful than anyone had ever known before or since? What *is* the explanation of this most terrible word: 'My God, my God, why hast thou forsaken me?'

Some people shrink from accepting the word which is so plainly set down. They say, 'God would not have forsaken His Son', or they say, 'It was a mistake on the part of Jesus. He only thought He was forsaken', or they say—and this I always find the most pitiful explanation of all—they say He was about to recite a psalm and was cut off after the first verse.

I am not unaware of the difficulties, though I do not feel

that they are adequately dealt with in any of those ways.

Jesus *said* this. It is here in the Gospels. It would never have been set down if it had not been said. It is the kind of word, I have no doubt, that the evangelist would like to have forgotten, but with burning honesty he puts it in. This awful cry of dereliction burst from the lips of Jesus when He hung on the Cross: 'My God, my God, why hast thou forsaken me?'

The people; the disciples; now God. He was lonelier than the loneliest.

Let us see if we can get a little nearer to the heart of this dark word.

III

I want to be quite frank and say I do not think anybody can plumb this awful mystery and make it completely clear. I do not regret that in a way. I would not expect as a mortal to be able to understand all the deep mystery of my redemption, but as I wander in the darkness at this point I carry in my hand a little lamp.

Paul lent me the lamp. It burns like this: 'Him who knew no sin, He made to be sin on our behalf.' Both truths are there in the text: 'Him who knew no sin, He made to be sin on our behalf.'

O! I know what you are saying. A dozen questions have leapt to your lips:

'How can anybody be made sin for somebody else?'

I don't know!

'How can the innocent suffer for the guilty?'

'I don't know!

'After all, sin can only be committed by oneself: how can it be placed on someone else?'

I don't know!

This I know: Paul said: 'Him who knew no sin, He made to be sin on our behalf.'

I hold that word before you. It goes beyond your understanding. You cannot fathom it. (Don't be too intimidated by that! We can experience things long before we can explain them. I enjoyed surf-bathing as a child for years without knowing that the moon had anything to do with it.) We are in the depths here, but hear it again. 'Him who knew no sin, He made to be sin on our behalf.'

The most awful thing about sin is the separation from God. I am sure of that. Even in my poor little way, if I lapse into sin, a cloud comes between God and my soul. My little fellowship is interrupted. There is a shadow on my communion. I become aware of it in the passing of a day or two. I ask myself, 'Why, why has this happened?' and I have no peace till I go to God about it.

And when I think, by analogy, of the intimate fellowship that Jesus enjoyed with His Father, I see that some dark cloud rolled between Him and God when He hung on the Cross. He knew no sin, and yet He entered into the experience of sin—the awful sense of separation from His Father. The cry of dereliction shows it. Whatever sin-bearing means, it means this; the consequences fell upon Him. 'Him who knew no sin, He made to be sin on our behalf.'

I have given much thought this week, even though I knew I couldn't really clear up the mystery for you, or for myself, to see if I could cast a little light upon it, and I want to do so now in two illustrations. They are simple; they are inadequate, and yet I hope that some light will fall on the mystery by this means.

The first is taken from medical science. During the first World War our authorities were greatly troubled by the trench-fever that was so affecting the soldiers, and they couldn't discover how it was communicated. The opinion had been expressed that it was spread by lice, and they sent for a remarkable man, a Mr Bacot, who had made a particular study of lice. They told him their need, and Mr Bacot went to work. He took the lice, put them into small pill-boxes with an aperture on the underside, and strapped them on his wrist beneath his cuffs. He let the evil things live on him. He went about his work receiving hundreds of bites a day, and the people who knew what he was doing saw him sitting in the tube trains with these slight bulges underneath his sleeve.

He began to get results. To save our men in their need he went to France, to Egypt, and to Poland too, exposing himself every day to hundreds of bites, and then testing out in his own body, when the infection was given, the power of a cure. Finally, he became completely infected with typhus and died. His story is just another of the splendid martyrdoms to science that our records hold.

He who was clean became unclean that he might save others. It is a poor parallel I know, but has it given you a little light?

Or let me take a more familiar instance—that of Father Damien. Father Damien was a Belgian missionary and he went to serve at Honolulu. Learning of the leper island of Molokai, and those six hundred poor unshepherded souls, he obtained permission to go and be the father and friend of them all. He went. He was dreadfully lonely on the island. You see, he was the only healthy man in an island made up entirely of lepers. The awful loneliness of it Damien confessed himself.

But one morning something happened. He was pouring some boiling water into a pan when some of it splashed on to his bare foot. He did not feel the pain. He looked at it for a moment in astonishment. It was boiling water and he did not feel the pain. And then the truth broke on him. One of the signs of the local leprosy was immunity to pain. He knew it in that moment of self-revelation. He

E

was a leper himself. A strange joy surged in his large heart. He rang his bell. He summoned his poor flock to church. He leapt into his pulpit. He spread his arms and said: 'Fellow lepers—fellow lepers——'

All analogies are poor. Both my little pictures fall far, far short of the truth. It remains true of our Lord that He 'knew no sin'. But brood on it yourself. Find better analogies if you can. 'Him who knew no sin, He made to be sin on our behalf.' He could never say 'fellow sinners', but He was made to be sin on our behalf.

> *The awful sorrow of His face,*
> *The bowing of His frame,*
> *Come not from torture nor disgrace:*
> *He fears not Cross nor shame.*
>
> *There is a deeper pang of grief,*
> *An agony unknown,*
> *In which His love finds no relief—*
> *He bears it all alone.*
>
> . . .
>
> *O may I in Thy sorrow share,*
> *And mourn, that sins of mine*
> *Should ever wound with grief or care*
> *That loving heart of Thine.*

7

He Honours an Ass

John 12¹⁴—*And Jesus, having found a young ass,*
sat thereon

I

THERE IS nothing dignified about a donkey. You
can look at him from any angle you like and you
will fail to find what men call 'presence'. He hasn't
got it. He is an awkward, obstinate, and, some have
thought, stupid beast. Indeed, the nature of the donkey
has passed into a proverb, and nobody supposes, if he is
called an 'ass', that the term is a term of endearment or a
mark of wisdom.

It is the presence of the donkey which makes Christ's
triumphal march the most peculiar thing of its kind in
history. Whoever heard of a conqueror riding in triumph
on an ass? If any Gentiles had been present when the
procession passed by, they must have been quietly
amused. To give a common donkey a prominent position
was enough to take the dignity out of any demonstration.
To the view of an outsider, it would have seemed absurd,
banal, ludicrous.

Not that it appeared in that light to the Jew! The Jews
were a peculiar people in many ways, and they were not
least peculiar in their burning love of peace. I think it is
a fact that only the Jews, of all the peoples of the ancient
world, conceived their early heroes as men of peace. If
this is true it is a piece of sociological information of
uncommon interest. All nations cherished stories about

their famous men of old—even though some of them may be mythical. And always, the famous men were men of *war*. Notice that!

Among the Norsemen we have the mighty vikings; in our own land we have the chivalrous stories of King Arthur and the knights of the Round Table. The Romans, Indians, and Japanese all tell the story of their early *warlike* heroes—and only the Jew conceived his early heroes as men of *peace*. Abraham, Isaac and Jacob, the three peerless patriarchs, were friends of God and lovers of peace. Isaac and Jacob never went to war at all, and Abraham only fought once, and then he was forced into it and, though he conquered, he took not a tithe of the spoil. It was this which affected the Hebrew Messianic hope. The Jews' ideal man was a man of peace, and when the Messiah came he would come in the accoutrements of peace; not on a prancing steed and with the blare of trumpets, but meekly, riding upon an ass.

And, as I have been looking again into that curious processional scene, I feel somehow that the donkey didn't let it down at all. So far from dragging the lowly pomp down to *his* level, he seems rather to have been drawn up to *its*. He has caught a strange dignity and quiet consciousness of privilege. The scene is not ludicrous but royal. The awkward, obstinate and despised beast, has been chosen by the Son of God, and he seems aware of his elevation. One might almost suppose that he had heard it said—'the Lord hath need of him'.

In his well-known poem on the donkey, G. K. Chesterton makes the donkey reply to those who sneer at him:

> *Fools! for I also had my hour,*
> *One far fierce hour and sweet;*
> *There was a shout about my ears*
> *And palms before my feet.*

And I see a parable in that. Whatever Christ touched He dignified, and no matter how despised a person or creature may be, Christ has a use for him. Let me say that again. No matter how ordinary, ill-educated, disfigured, ill-born, one-talented or obscure a man or woman may be, Christ has a use for them, and He gives them dignity by that use.

Let me illustrate that in every case.

II

1. *He uses ordinary people.* Consider His use of the disciples themselves. They were all ordinary men. So far as we know, there wasn't a high-born man among them, nor a genius, nor a scholar. We know the occupation of only five out of the twelve. Four were fishermen and one was a tax-collector—though a tax-collector in those days corresponded more to a greedy moneylender in our modern life than to a respected government official. And with that group of ordinary men, Christ turned the world upside down!

He has been using ordinary men ever since and doing mighty things with them. He does not work only with the geniuses. He will work with anybody who will give Him a consecrated heart. He is displeased with those who shrink away from His call, cuddling their inferiorities and saying: 'I'm not clever, or saintly, or ten-talented. I can't do anything.' The Christ who made use of a despised animal could make greater use of you and, if He doesn't, it will be because you won't let Him.

2. *He uses the ill-educated.* Education comes in various ways. I have never been able to decide whether I learnt more in the army or at the university—from men or from books. The experiences, I have often felt, were complementary.

But when we talk of education we normally mean the best schooling our society provided at the time and all through the years Christ has made mighty use of people denied that quality of education. Think of John Bunyan, the tinker, and William Carey, the shoe-maker, and William Booth, the pawnbroker's assistant. Each of them was a highly intelligent man. It was only formal schooling that they lacked—and how the academic world scorned them for that lack! What things the scholars said about Bunyan—though he wrote the greatest allegory in the English tongue. What sneers Carey endured—though he influenced the life of all India. What contempt was poured on Booth (*The Times* always put his rank in quotes; 'General' Booth.) though he raised a multi-racial army to march in Christ's Name all round the world.

3. *He uses the disfigured*—and those disfigured in the ways the ignorant find amusing. Think of Henry Martyn with his wart-covered face and his stammer, and George Whitefield with his enormous and grotesque squint. Poor Martyn was the butt of cheap jokes at school, at Cambridge, and in India too. We do not even know the names of those who made such ill-considered fun of him, but *his* name grows more lustrous with passing years. The writer hardly exaggerated who called him 'the most heroic figure in the English Church in 400 years'.

And how they laughed on Kennington Common when Whitefield stood up to preach. If he made the mistake of saying, 'That man. That man I am looking at now,' two men always came under conviction!

But what did it matter? Cross-eyed or not, Christ made mighty use of George Whitefield.

4. *He uses the ill-born*. All normal people are sad if they learn that their birth was out of wedlock, but what mighty use Christ has made of some of them.

Think of Alexander Whyte, the great Puritan preacher of Scotland a generation ago and (some would think) one of Scotland's modern saints as well. He was illegitimate. Don't hasten to make the modern comment, 'There are no illegitimate children; only illegitimate parents,' because—as all testified—Alexander Whyte's mother was essentially a good woman, not to be forever stained by this known sin.

What wonderful use the Saviour made of that 'improper' child! What multitudes hung on his preaching; were blessed by his books; humbled by his humility.

Christ has a special sympathy with those on the circumstances of whose birth this kind of shadow falls. He wants them to know that He is greater than ancestry. His own 'birth-roll' includes some odd names. Ruth— the Moabitess! What do the apostles of racial purity make of that? Rahab the harlot!—in the 'birth-roll' of the Son of God!

Don't let any secret shame about your family history make you feel unfit to answer His call. You *are* unfit no doubt—we *all* are!—but when He calls, leap to obey.

5. *He uses the one-talented.* Never forget that it was the *one*-talented man who was rebuked in the parable. If you are one-talented or half-talented, beware of apeing humility. They often go together. 'What can I do? I have so little!' Little or much, you will come to the last Audit like everyone else. Christ has done mighty things with one-talented men and women.

Most people who knew him put Phillip Bliss in that category. He was no poet. He had a single simple gift of versification and he put it on the altar.

What use the Saviour made of it! All round the English-speaking world people sang his gospel songs— and some do still. He reached people preachers couldn't touch. Housewives did their washing with his lilting words on their lips and many millions in this past century learned to 'shout, shout the sound'.

6. *He uses obscure people.* Who was the farm labourer who clambered up a pyramid of his fellows to lift John Wesley as a little boy of six from the blazing rectory at Epworth on 9th February 1709? Did he affect the spiritual history of the world? I think he did. Nobody knows his name.

Who was the preacher who in Colchester in June 1850 constrained Charles Haddon Spurgeon to 'look and live'? After much research I am sure I know, but I sometimes think that there aren't a hundred people in the world who do.

Did he affect the religious history of Britain? Who can doubt it?

So we could go on, but does it really require this re-duplication of instances? Yet I wanted to cover you all. To which group do you belong?—ordinary? ill-educated? disfigured? ill-born? one-talented? obscure?

The Christ who made splendid use on Palm Sunday of an ass can make a higher use of you.

III

Now, I am aware that some of you will half-resent my reasoning and not feel flattered at this recurrent comparison with an ass.

Why not? I am comparing myself as well. Haven't you been stubborn on occasion?—stupid?—undignified? I have been all three—and not seldom. Certainly I don't feel too superior to learn on this day in the Christian year from that honoured ass.

I wonder if you know Carisbrooke Castle in the Isle of Wight. It is famous (among other things) as the one-time prison of Charles I. They have a donkey there and I have many times patted his back. The donkey works in a little round house and his whole task is to go round, and round, and round. That is all he does. He has no particular stopping- or starting-place. He just goes round, and round, and round.

Put your head in the door and take a glance. He's still going round, and round, and round. What's the use of it, you say? Is there any purpose at all in the gyrations of the poor beast? Yes! There is. He's drawing the water. The well is deep at Carisbrooke Castle. Very deep! And that poor beast is not walking in circles for nothing. He's drawing the water. You can get a cold drink on a sweltering day by the aid of that donkey at Carisbrooke Castle. It sometimes takes discernment to see the use of lowly labours.

And I have known obscure and lowly Christians who knew how to give one a drink of the divine water when the tongue was parched; living monotonous and humdrum lives, but wise in the wisdom of God. A young woman of the smart set spoke critically to me once about the people in my church. She thought they were all thoroughly stale and old-fashioned: 'Look at old Mr Aslett,' she said, 'What does he know about life; life with a capital L?'

I did what she told me. I thought on old Mr Aslett. He was a simple man in some ways, but I remembered the time when his three children were smitten with scarlet fever together, and two of them died in one day. I remembered his faith in that midnight hour. I remembered why he was still a *poor* man; because he would not compromise his conscience on a certain point, and missed making a large sum of money. I remembered how often the old man had cheered me in my work by his simple and loving testimony to Jesus.

He looked like a poor old ass to the smart young thing; turning in monotonous circles and doing nothing, but if she only knew it he was drawing living water from the wells of the Spirit of God.

So may we! All's well! It's Palm Sunday and one message of Palm Sunday is this: that the Lord who gave dignity and prominence to a despised beast will give place and honour even to such unimportant people as are we. The world may not know our name, but we dare believe that it is written in the Lamb's Book of Life.

8

He Dies. He *must* Die

Luke 24²⁶—*Behoved it not the Christ to suffer these things?*

WE OFTEN SPEAK of the Cross as stark and unrelieved tragedy; as the most awful, wicked, and incongruous thing which ever happened on this planet. And, in a sense, we are right. Almighty God comes to earth, lives as a man among men . . . and He is whipped, spat upon, pierced with nails, and hung up naked for leprous sinners and painted harlots to jeer at. It is too shocking to be credible.

> *He laid His glory by,*
> *He wrapped Him in our clay;*
> *Unmarked by human eye,*
> *The latent Godhead lay.*

And when *He* did that, *we*

> *. . . set at nought and sold Him,*
> *Pierced and nailed Him to the tree.*

I marvel that even in hell they could think of anything so fiendishly wicked as that. It was, indeed, the most incongruous thing which ever happened on this planet.

And yet, while that is true, it is only half the truth. In all the awful incongruity, I perceive a congruity as well. In the midst of its shocking unfitness, I see a fitness too. A *fitness* in the Cross! I learnt it from my Lord Himself in the first explanation He ever made about His dying after He had risen from the dead. Walking to Emmaus with two disciples who did not recognize Him and who were stunned by all that happened on Calvary, He was at pains to explain to them *why the Cross had to be*. He said: 'Behoved it not the Christ to suffer these things?' Can't you see the fittingness of it? Don't you see that it is the keystone of the arch?

And when I got that word from Jesus, I raced through the rest of the New Testament to find confirmation in other parts of Scripture for the interpretation I gave to that word. The confirmation was there. I started with the Epistle to the Hebrews and I read of Jesus: 'It behoved Him in all things to be made like unto His brethren.' He *had* to suffer. It *behoved* Him. I should have guessed it.

I read of the Father in the same Epistle: 'It became Him to make the author of their salvation perfect through suffering.' It *became* Him. It was fitting.

So there it is. The sublime paradox again. A great crime; a great love. A vast incongruity; a lovely congruity. The world's worst; Heaven's best.

> *O love of God! O sin of man!*
> *In this dread act your strength is tried;*
> *And victory remains with love:*
> *For He, our Lord, is crucified.*

And then, I look still farther afield to find confirmation of this truth. John Wesley, as you may recall, had two simple tests for any teaching he gave to people, and he expected the tests to corroborate each other. 'Is it in the Bible?' he asked first. And then: 'Is it in experience?'

I find this strange teaching of the fittingness of the Cross in the Bible. Can I find that teaching in life as well?

I find it in life as well! Sacrifice is written all over life. It runs like a scarlet thread through all our racial history and all our personal history too. The Cross isn't a queer incongruity which occurred in history only on the first Good Friday. To those who have insight, it has been in this strange life of ours from the beginning. What did the author of the Book of Revelation mean when he said 'A Lamb slain from the foundation of the world'? The Cross is *in* life: *all* life. It has been in life from the beginning; from the foundation of the world. It is, indeed, so much in life that you could call it the foundation itself, the ground-plan of the universe. Our life is all reared on a Cross.

I once took a small boy into a cathedral. We entered by the west door, and as our eyes grew accustomed to the dim light, he looked up above the rood-screen and he said: 'There is a Cross up there.' I pointed to the floor of the cathedral and said: 'There is a Cross down here.' The cathedral was a Cross. Of course! It was a cruciform building. Chancel and nave for the upright; transept and transept for the cross-beam. It was all Cross.

You can take me to Golgotha and say: 'There is a Cross up there.' I point you to the earth and say: 'There is a Cross down here.' The Cross is inherent in life. It is life's foundation. It is not an incongruity. Your Saviour is focusing in a moment of time a fact which is timeless, and on the first Good Friday the Lamb slain from the foundation of the world is *seen* slain. What a mystery! How shall we pierce into the heart of this?

The Cross is in all life. It is in the earth; the seed dies that the plant may live. It is in the landscape; the mountain is bare and barren that the vale may be rich and fecund. 'The valleys stand so thick with corn . . .' Aye, they do! And they do it by the soil washed from the mountain. The Cross is in your blood. What are the white corpuscles doing in your blood-stream? Watching for infection! When they find it, they absorb it, but they too, in their turn, must be absorbed by the newly created cells which take their place, or the blood would stagnate and the body would die.

I say again: the Cross is not one vast incongruity. It is the red element in all life, but in Jesus on the Cross it is placarded before your eyes. It has a terrible fitness in this world. Listen to Him explaining it Himself to those two men on the way to Emmaus: 'Behoved it not the Christ to suffer these things?' Wasn't it fitting? Could it have been avoided?

It couldn't have been avoided. Not by the Saviour.

> *He did not come to judge the word,*
> *He did not come to blame;*
> *He did not only come to seek,*
> *It was to save He came;*
> *And when we call Him Saviour,*
> *Then we call Him by His Name.*

Let us see if we can understand a little more clearly why the Cross was necessary. We shall not understand it all. The deep mystery will elude our probing, but some gleam of understanding will come as we gaze.

I will put it to you as questions.

I

Could any but a crucified Saviour reveal our sins?

It is a recurrent tragedy of our race that we do not realize the sinfulness of sin. We call our sins 'mistakes', 'weaknesses', 'slips', and even when we use the right word —'sin'—we use it lightly. What is sin?

This is sin! It is sin that takes the holy God—incarnate here on earth—and treats Him as no beast should be treated. It is sin that takes the gracious loving Jesus, who never harmed a soul and spent all His days in helping and healing, and strips Him, lashes Him, spits on Him, pierces Him with nails ... and then laughs at Him. That is sin. Your sin. O yes! *your* sin. You have been guilty of the same sins which nailed Him to the Cross. Gossip, greed, bigotry, fear, slander ... they added up to this. You have gossiped, been greedy, bigoted, fearful, and slanderous. You didn't think it came to this in the end. It took the Cross to make you realize what sin really was.

Sin is deadly. It is the one thing God won't tolerate. The war between good and evil is to the death. And you lend yourself to sin without knowing to what dirty enterprise you have sold yourself ... *until you see that Cross.*

Whenever you are tempted to feel that it is only a 'white lie'; whenever you catch yourself saying: 'Well, one must look after oneself'; whenever you are greedy, slanderous, loose in speech, selfish and grasping ... look at the Cross. That shows its real nature. Sin isn't an invention of preachers. Sin does that ... and you would never have known its deadly nature had He not endured to be placarded before your eyes.

Have you ever seen the germs which cause disease magnified for examination? They are most interesting to look at. They have such curious shapes; even beautiful shapes, some of them. It is possible to take an artist's interest in them and half forget the deadly nature they possess.

But now go straight from that magnified specimen-glass and see the germ at its deadly work in the hospital ward. Look!—this is *Lupus* at work. You were specially drawn to that magnified bacillus. It seemed so innocent; even pleasing to look upon.

Yet that germ is doing this; it is eating that man's living flesh away. On and on it goes and nothing, it seems, can arrest it. You didn't know the deadly character of that bacillus when you first looked at it. It seemed just 'cute', and you could discuss it with academic detachment. But what does it do? It does this!

So it is with sin. You *can* discuss it academically. You can even argue whether there is such a thing or not, or whether it is all the imagination of moralists.

But then go and look at the Cross. It does that. It is the most deadly thing known to God and man. It would slay the body and damn the soul. It is hell's worst. You can see it when you gaze upon the Cross.

II

Here is my second question:

Could any but a crucified Saviour save *us from our sins?*

It seems not. The New Testament is quite emphatic upon the point. Without shedding of blood there is no remission. It is death which gives life.

Now, why that should be I do not know, and I don't think anybody else does but God Himself. The New Testament has no theories about the Atonement. It has the Atonement—but not an explanation.

That is often the case in the Bible. The Bible begins right away by talking about God. 'In the beginning, God . . .', but it never sets out to prove Him. The Bible everywhere assumes man's moral freedom, but nowhere does it seek to explain it. The Bible always speaks with authority of God's Book, but never self-consciously. It never sets out to prove by argument that it is a Book apart.

And so with the Atonement. It is there. Plain. Repeated. Emphatic. Without shedding of blood there is no remission. But it never says 'why'.

I wonder if that hint I gave just now will give us the clue that we are seeking? The Cross is inherent in all life. No life without death. There is sacrifice woven into the very fabric of our days. It is in the earth; it is in the landscape; it is in our blood . . . all life illustrates and reaches out for that divine principle in the universe. It is here eternally in God. You may see it in a moment of time. The Lamb slain from the foundation of the world is *seen* slain, and by His stripes we are healed.

Find time during this solemn day to sit quietly before the Cross. Just sit and look and meditate on the Passion hymns.

> *Five bleeding wounds He bears,*
>   *Received on Calvary;*
> *They pour effectual prayers,*
>   *They strongly speak for me:*
> *Forgive him, O forgive! they cry,*
> *Nor let that ransomed sinner die!*

You see? It is the bleeding wounds which cry.

> *Forgive him, O forgive! they cry,*
> *Nor let that ransomed sinner die!*

> *O let me kiss Thy bleeding feet,*
>   *And bathe and wash them with my tears!*
> *The story of Thy love repeat*
>   *In every drooping sinner's ears,*
> *That all may hear the quickening sound,*
> *Since I, even I, have mercy found.*

And, as you sit and gaze, it will be borne in upon you that only a crucified Saviour could meet your need.

Canon Peter Green tells of how he came out of his church in Salford one day and saw a young working man staring incredulously at a crucifix, and, seeing the parson, the young man said: 'I don't see what good it done the Father that His Son should die like that.'

What a confusion of ideas lies behind that remark. It wasn't the good of the Father; it was the good of undone sinners that led our Lord to die upon the wood. And, in His well-beloved Son, the Father suffered too. If you say that God required the penalty, you must at least say that

God paid it. Make no division in the Godhead. It is bound to be false.

> For you and for me
> He prayed on the tree:
> The prayer is accepted, the sinner is free.
> That sinner am I,
> Who on Jesus rely,
> And come for the pardon God cannot deny.

III

Here is my third question.

Could any but a crucified Saviour meet us in our agony?

I have learned nothing in more than thirty years of ministry if I have not learned that there are tears in things. When life is at the spring and love is young and one is fit, how sweet and engaging life seems. Anybody who takes a sombre view of life is thought to be a dull pessimist unable to see this lovely life as it is.

Those who see this life as it is see the tears in things. Enjoy it while you can. Seize every scrap of legitimate happiness, but remember . . . life is not a picnic. There are tears in things.

Every day the undertaker plies his solemn trade. Every day hearts break. Every day the routine goes on in a thousand hospitals; the cancer hospitals; the homes for blind babies; the homes for the epileptics . . . and on and on it goes. You who are healthy and happy; you can forget those things. I am glad, in a way, you can. But those of us who see life whole, we cannot.

I was in Macclesfield a while ago and as we ran through the town I was impressed by a great institution: one part of it so modern, with colourful green tiles, and one part of it old; but all of it so extensive. It seemed to take the car quite a while to pass by. 'What a place!' I said to my friends. 'What a *huge* place!'

'Yes,' they said. 'It is the mental hospital.'

The *mental* hospital! That saddest of all sicknesses. There are tears in things.

Every week the minister must meet the broken-hearted. I say again: *you* may forget it; *we* can't.

If I had no crucified Saviour with which to greet those who have been broken by the tragedies of life, I would not know what to say to them. How could I speak to that girl whose young husband was actually killed on their honeymoon? How could I speak to those parents whose longed-for child turned out to be a cretin? How could I speak to that poor polio victim twenty years in an iron lung? How could one speak to the multitude of sufferers in a world like this if one had no crucified Saviour to speak about?

To all those whose minds reel in sorrow; to all those who feel resentful because life has done to them its worst; to all those tempted to believe there is no God in Heaven, or, at least, no God of love, He comes and He shows them His hands. More eloquently than any words those pierced hands say: 'I have suffered.'

There are tears in things . . . and there were tears on the face of Jesus Christ. Not for His own suffering, but for that of others, is it not recorded that Jesus wept?

He weeps with the sufferers still; with you who are suffering, and whose hearts may be bitter and resentful, even while I speak to you.

You can't steel yourself against this suffering life. You need the 'inside word' He brings. Can you resist the appeal of those eyes 'majestic after death'?

He has suffered. He knows the answers. He could bring even you to utter peace.

'Behoved it not the Christ to suffer these things?' Wasn't it fitting? Can't you see it *had* to be?

9

He Rises Again

Mark 16⁴—*The stone was rolled away*

IT IS A painfully small ministry that can be exercised upon the body of our dead—yet love always insists on offering it. The last sad offices are performed with a studious care which shows how keenly our broken hearts bewail the finality of service; a clod is precious that has housed a much-loved soul.

Even the deserted and crucified Son of God had dear ones who were anxious to offer this last expression of devotion to Him. There were women who set out early for the place of His burial. Their eagerness is shown in the manner of their coming. Mark and Luke tell us that they were hastening to the sepulchre 'very early in the morning'. Matthew says 'as it began to dawn'. John says 'when it was yet dark'—these women came bearing the spices in their hands; blessedly zealous over the useless; with the desperation of love, which *will* find service, they came to make that wearied body restful for the long night of death.

Nor is their haste shown only by the hour of their coming. It is revealed, also, in the very composition of the party. There was no man in it!—and the sepulchre was sealed with a stone and the stone was 'very great'. Perhaps they hardly thought of this in their hasty departure, but it came to them on the way and they murmured to one another, 'Who shall roll us away the stone from the door of the tomb?' Then they arrive! . . . *and the stone is rolled away! . . . and the sepulchre is empty* . . . and a white-robed youth addresses them: 'Be not amazed: ye seek Jesus, the Nazarene which hath been crucified. He is risen: He is not here: Behold the place where they laid Him.' And the women fled from the tomb in astonishment, trembling, speechless and afraid.

That was the most glorious dawn in human history! There was a radiance in the golden light of that morning the world had never known before.

I

Let us explore the heart of this sublime event with three questions—questions which may seem a little naïve when you first hear them. Here is the first. *What stone was rolled away?*

Make no effort to hide the fact. Death is the great enigma of life. Humanly speaking, it is an insoluble mystery; it is the one secret of the universe which is kept; the silence which is never broken. Death is one of the rare things which can be predicted of all men; the common end to a path of glory or a road of shame. To the weary and despairing it may come as a friend; the cynical and disillusioned may meet it with indifference; to the healthy and happy it may appear as a foe, but as friend, or foe, or cold companion, it comes to all. All our plans for the future are made subject to its approval. There is no earthly tie too sacred for death to loosen. It reduces the exalted and the lowly to the common denominator of dust.

Moreover, the mystery is as old as mankind. From the dimmest beginnings of history, we find men pondering the problem of the beyond. In the upward movement of mankind we find them nursing their hopes on a variety of dreams, and passing in turn from belief in a dim spirit life to the shadowy existence called Sheol, and finally to the vision of a life fuller and grander than this. But it was still a mystery. These dreams were . . . *dreams*; interesting speculations, but nothing more. Death was still 'the undiscovered country from whose bourn no traveller returns'. This was the great stone that blocked the path of human aspiration. What certitude was there of the continuity of life? What modest man could find in himself anything worthy to endure for all eternity? Of what abiding worth was love even—our highest—if it ended in the passionless calm of death?

Then came the first Easter Day and—*the stone was rolled away!* That stone! Mark says it was 'exceeding heavy'. And now it is rolled away, for one Traveller returned. Death is an abysmal cavern no more, but a tunnel with a golden light at the farther end. It is no more a blind alley, but a thoroughfare; no more a cul-de-sac, but a highway. The mystery is a mystery no more. ''Tis Death is dead, not He.' 'And', says Paul, 'if the Spirit of Him that raised up Jesus from the dead dwell in you, He that raised up Jesus from the dead shall quicken also your mortal bodies by His spirit that dwelleth in you.'

The stone is rolled away and justifies the blessed contradictoriness of the phrase in the burial service, 'the sure and certain hope [a *certain hope?*] of everlasting life'.

II

Here is the second question. *Why was the stone rolled away?*

Surely it was not rolled away that the Risen Lord might come out? Of whatever nature was His resurrection body, the Lord Jesus was independent of doors and indifferent to walls. John explicitly tells us: 'Jesus cometh, the doors being shut, and stood in the midst and said, Peace be unto you.' And yet the stone was rolled away! I think I know why. It was not rolled away that

He might come out, but that they might go in. It was no part of the *fact;* it was a part merely of the *demonstration.* It was not the means of His exit, but the means of their entrance. This it is that makes the resurrection more than a piece of history; it makes it also a pledge. This lifts it above the level of mere news and makes it a promise, for God rolled away the stone, not that His Son might rise, but that we might know He had risen; that we might steal into the empty tomb and see only 'the place where they laid Him'.

Do I make the distinction clear? Let me illustrate! Let us suppose that a child was entrusted to my care and it fell to my lot one night to put him to bed. I would take him, I suppose, to his room and hear his prayers and tuck him in . . . with all the good intention and all the awkwardness of a mere man. And then, as I am about to leave the room and take the light with me, suppose the little fellow falteringly confesses a childish fear to me; tells me that he lives in dread of the other side of that dark and heavy curtain in the corner; that he is foolishly afraid that there is something evil on the farther side, and in the darkness he can almost see some sinister shape emerge to do him harm. . . .

Well! I could leave the room with one peremptory word in my adult awareness that his fear is baseless . . . but I am far too concerned about his peace of mind for that. So I go to the shadowed corner of the room and fling the curtain aside, and flood the dark recess with light and show the groundlessness of his fears; smile the assurance of my love upon him and say: 'See? There is *nothing* to fear.' My removal of the curtain is no part of the removal of evil, but it is part of the removal of his dread. I have come down to his level that he may find peace, and I am rewarded by seeing him fall calmly asleep.

So God rolled away the stone! It was not necessary for the resurrection of the Lord, but it was necessary for its wider publication. It wasn't necessary that Christ might rise, but it was an impressive and unforgettable part of the proclamation of that fact.

III

Here is the third question. *What did that rolled-away stone reveal?*

Let us follow the women into the tomb. It is a great hole, you see, hewn in a rock. What? Do you shrink a little because it is a tomb? Did you say it makes you feel eerie?

Not here! Not in the *Saviour's* tomb! It's empty! There's nothing to be seen: only *the place where they laid Him*.

What went you out to see?

Nothing!

Nothing? Were you satisfied?

It was the most glorious moment of my life.

Amongst the several accounts we have of this tomb let us follow most closely the account given in the Fourth Gospel. You cannot doubt, I think, that behind this record there is the clear testimony of an eyewitness. Peter and John run together to the tomb. John outruns Peter yet hesitates to go in. Peter pants up behind, but doesn't hesitate for a moment. In he goes and John follows him. When they are standing together in the sepulchre they see the linen clothes lying and 'the napkin that was about His head not lying with the linen clothes but wrapped together in a place by itself'.

Some scholars have sensed a strange overtone in the Greek word used to describe the head-cloth. I will be frank and say that I do not get the flavour from the Greek myself, but I am glad to share with you what others savour—or think they savour—even when I don't quite get it myself. Some scholars say that the word used about the head-cloth suggests that it still had an annular shape. It was lying apart from the other clothes and still had the outline of His head—the sacred head once wounded—

With grief and pain weighed down—

still had the form of that 'dear disfigured face', the visage more marred than any man's.

Do you get the picture? This is the account of an eyewitness. Does it almost make you feel that you are an eyewitness yourself? Can you see it happen? This was no laborious unwinding! This was a glorious uprising!!

And all alone alone alone,
He rose again behind the stone.

How calm and private that blessed sepulchre must have been after all the dreadful and shameful publicity of the Crucifixion. How quiet and still! How blessedly secluded. Jesus loved solitude and He had no solitude between Gethsemane and the sepulchre. Working out the time is difficult, but it seems that eight hours after His arrest He was on the Cross. Eight awful hours! In the brief space of six hours He was examined five times by four different tribunals. In all the haste of their fiendish cruelty they rushed Him from Annas—to Caiaphas —to Pilate—to Herod and back to Pilate again—and then to the Cross. Oh! having driven in the nails and done their devilest, why couldn't they let Him die in quietness and in the company of His dear ones? But no! The cup must be drunk to the dregs and the ghastly publicity of it was part of the bitterness of the Cross.

So as He hangs there—the noise, the dust, the pain, the thirst—and perhaps the incessant noise was not the least of His pangs, the crowds, the jeers, the curses, the sobbing women—and He hangs stark naked between earth and heaven.

O for quietness; for solitude; only to be alone. Through His swimming eyes He sees His mother's face. It brings Nazareth back to Him. Childhood and the fields of Galilee. And John is there. Dear John! 'Woman, behold thy son. Son, behold thy mother.' And still the noise . . . raucous laughter and bitter sobbing . . . until the blessed numbness steals over His outworn frame . . . and then . . .

'It is finished! Father, into Thy hands I commend my spirit.'

And then the sepulchre. Do you still think of a tomb as being cold and eerie? No! No! It is quiet, and calm, and our crucified God rests for hours and hours on a cool bed of rock.

And then (to quote Alice Meynell again):

> *All alone alone alone,*
> *He rose again behind the stone.*

10

He Tarries Among Us

Acts 1³—*To whom He also shewed himself alive after his passion by many proofs, appearing unto them by the space of forty days, and speaking the things concerning the kingdom of God*

FORTY DAYS divided the Resurrection and the Ascension. What a wonderful forty days they must have been for the Apostles! There was first the almost intolerable ache of joy in their hearts as the wonderful truth slowly mastered the lifelong conviction that dead men do not live again. There was, also, the delirious hope every morning that, at any moment, Christ might appear to them, and another proof be added to the accumulating evidence that He was, indeed, alive for evermore. Most of all there were the actual appearances themselves, the teaching and the reminders; the promises and the admonitions.

I think—had I been one of them—that what would have impressed me most would have been my own incredible dullness in the days before Calvary. Again and again, I fancy, it would have risen in my bewildered memory: 'Yes. He did say that. "The Son of Man must be delivered into the hands of sinful men and be crucified, and after three days rise from the dead." It comes back to me now. How could I have been so dull? I must have been thinking of something else—what I was going to get out of it when He was made King—and in my selfishness I let Him go to His death misunderstood and alone. . . .' What a wonderful forty days they must have been for the Apostles!

But what were they for Jesus? What was the divine purpose in that more-than-a-month between His rising on earth and His rising to Heaven? What was unfinished in the work, or incomplete in the training of the disciples, that could still deny Him the full enjoyment of His Father's home above?

That is the question I should like us to face to-day.

I

I think He tarried among them *first*, to *leave them in no doubt about the Resurrection.*

The Authorized Version says that our Lord showed Himself alive after His passion by many *infallible* proofs. The Revisers dropped the word 'infallible' and let 'proofs' stand in its own unbuttressed strength. The truth, I think, is between the two. The Greek word would sustain (in my judgement) some such adjective as 'definite' or 'convincing', though the point is not important. If a proof *is* a proof, it is enough.

And this, at least, cannot be in question. The proofs were numerous. He came—and came again!

Some things are so incredible that we find them hard to believe though all our senses testify that they are true.

Do you remember the little girl visiting the zoo and seeing an elephant for the first time? She stared at the huge bulk, and flapping ears, and elongated nose of the mighty mammal and said quite definitely: 'I don't believe it.' There are times when the mind refuses the clear judgement of the senses.

Did you ever receive a letter which contained such wonderful news that you couldn't believe it? 'It's too good to be true,' you said (as if *anything* could be too good to be true in a world which belongs to the God and Father of our Lord Jesus Christ!). You read the letter over and over again.

Forgive a personal illustration taken from my student days.

I remember sitting an important examination at the University and having a poor time with a paper on Greek composition. I knew the rules. 'Fail in one paper and you fail in all.' I sadly wiped even hope out of my heart and didn't bother to note the date when the results would be published.

Then one morning I received a telegram from my tutor with the single word: 'Congratulations.'

'I can't believe it,' I said to my friend with whom I was spending the vacation, and he replied: 'Let's go to the University and see the lists for ourselves.'

We went at once . . . and there was my name. I still didn't believe it.

'Do you see it too?' I said to my friend, and he laughingly assured me that he saw it too.

Walking back to the station on air, I was suddenly assailed by doubt again. Sheepishly, I said to my friend: 'Let's go back and look at it again.'

Well . . . that's human nature! I say again that some things are so wonderful that we can't take them in, and nothing in all history (after the Incarnation) was so wonderful as our Lord's rising from the dead.

If He had appeared to them on one day only, they would have doubted it afterwards themselves. They would have said: 'It was an illusion. We were overwrought. We only imagined it. . . .'

So He tarried among them. So He piled up the proof. Mary. Peter. Two going to Emmaus. Ten disciples together. Eleven disciples. James. On one occasion five hundred at once.

Day succeeded day, and week succeeded week, and, when the forty days were gone, no doubt remained in any of their minds.

It *couldn't* be—and yet it *was!* Dead men don't rise again, but *this* Man *did!* 'We will announce this news to all the ages,' said the Apostles. 'On our honest testimony multi-millions yet unborn will rely.'

He arose! Hallelujah! Christ arose!

II

Here is the *second* reason why I think our Lord tarried. He tarried that *the disciples might learn a new independence*.

When Jesus was with them all the time they could refer every question to His immediate judgement. 'What shall we do about the tribute money, Lord?' 'What shall we do about these Samaritans who will not give us hospitality in their village?' 'What shall we do about this poor epileptic boy?'

And it is clear that people who can turn for an authoritative ruling on every difficult question don't grow beyond a certain point. Sooner or later the wise teacher stands a hand's-breadth off and nurtures independence by strengthening individual judgement.

It is so in our human relations. We only learnt to walk when we were babies because our mothers let us go, took the willing risk, and watched our tottering feet make towards the goal.

It was so when we came to the years of manhood and womanhood. The day came when we had to leave home. There may have been some shrinking in our minds from the ordeal and something of unwillingness on our parents' part to let us go, but *we* knew, and *they* knew, that in most cases it is necessary for the fullest development, and we learnt most when we stood alone.

To such a point had the Apostles now come. They were to be helped supremely by the gift of the Holy Spirit, but the Spirit's help was to be received and interpreted through human faculties and those faculties were to be exercised by independent use. Mistakes would be made. Paul would differ from Peter and Peter from Paul; differ so strongly that a sharp contention would arise between them, and two men, both of whom believed that they were guided by the Holy Spirit, would find themselves diametrically opposed. God took that risk. We may say reverently: 'God *had* to take that risk.' Growth is only possible by a measure of independence. People who don't develop their own judgement remain at the mental age of sixteen. Jesus was schooling His men to world evangelism and to all the solemn responsibilities of spreading the Church. And He did it in part by this gradual withdrawal. They had to learn to think and act for themselves. Not daily, but only at intervals, could they listen now to His spoken words. And at the end of forty days He was to vanish from their sight for ever.

Notice that. It will comfort you in some of the perplexities of these present times. No honest person among us will deny that there are times when we long for an authoritative ruling straight from the lips of Christ. 'Lord, tell us plainly; should we never take up arms in the fight against evil, and should we oppose it only by our thoughts, our testimony, and our prayers?' 'Lord, tell us plainly, are we right to limit trade with people whose politics we disapprove?' 'Lord, tell us plainly, is racial segregation always and everywhere wrong?' 'Lord, Lord!'

There it is. The longing in human hearts for a plain and authoritative ruling; a shrinking from the burden of laboured thought.

And God will not exempt us. He will think *with* us, but not *for* us. He treats us as persons and not puppets; as men and women and not marionettes; as free beings and not automatons. To His growing children, He does not say: 'Do this, do that.' He says rather: 'My child, stand at My side; glimpse My purposes; see My heart; work *with* Me, and together we will bring the Kingdom in.'

Take comfort in your perplexities. The Apostles walked this way, and walked this way by God's will. Better so! Better by far that we do God's will because we see the rightness of it than that we do God's will in blind obedience to a greater power.

Let me put it in a picture for you.

Are you a father? How old is your son? Six? Eight? Ten?

I suppose you realize that your boy when he grows up might go wrong. You can't open a newspaper today without reading of youth astray. He might get a girl into trouble. He might become a thief—a thug even. You've thought of that?

Of course you have!

There is one condition on which your boy could never go wrong: never be apprehended by the police; would always do what you told him . . . one simple condition . . . that he was a moron; that he remained all his life at the age of eight; that he never became independent.

And you say at once: '*Not that!* Whatever the risk, let my boy grow up; let him be normal. Let him be fully intelligent, self-disciplined and self-directing. . . .'

Well, that was part of our Lord's problem, and one reason, I think, why He tarried on earth—to school the disciples to a new independence.

III

The third great lesson the apostles had to learn was this. *Fellowship does not depend on a body.* Fellowship is really a companionship of minds. It can be independent of a body; it can never be independent of a mind.

Let me prove that to you. It is easily possible for people to see plainly the *forms* of other folk, to know their names

and where they live and what they like to eat, and yet have
no real fellowship with them because they have no fellowship with their minds. It is just as possible for people who
have never seen the forms of other people (who lived,
maybe, long before them in point of time) to hold
fellowship with them because they know their minds.

I was talking recently with a nurse from a mental
hospital. (I do not think the average person in the
community realizes how much we owe to nurses, both
male and female, in our *mental* hospitals. I hazard the
opinion, after much visitation in hospitals, that no work
that is done for the community is more costly and splendid
than this.)

The girl to whom I was speaking explained to me at
some length that, of course, she had no fellowship with
the minds of her patients. They were chronic cases. She
cared for their bodies; she asked God's help never to get
hard; she was patient and loving with them; she knew
them well, their names and their preferences and their
tastes, and their little idiosyncrasies; but, of course, she
could have no real fellowship at all. Her patients' minds
were far less clear than the minds of bright children.
She could *never* be intimate with them at all.

And when I asked her how she managed to keep so
bright and cheerful, she explained at once that it all
came out of fellowship, not with anybody she could see,
but with Someone whose mind she knew and whose
heart she loved. She smiled at me and said:

> *My God, is any hour so sweet,*
> *From blush of morn to evening star,*
> *As that which calls me to Thy feet,*
> *The hour of prayer?*

You see my point? She could have no fellowship with the
people whose bodies she was constantly serving: she had

G

the sweetest and richest fellowship with One she had never seen.

Or look at it another way. I was talking to a soldier the other day who seems to have got into a company of men whose minds are all out of tune with his own. 'The only talk they have', he said, 'are bawdy stories, filthy and horrible things which I am compelled to hear because they shout the foul details to one another across the hut. I am trying to prevent a barrier growing up between us. I don't want to be either a snob or a prig, but I cannot honestly say that I have any real fellowship with them. I long for the hour when work is done and I can get to my books, Robertson's *Sermons* and Lacordaire's *Life*, which I am just reading, and, of course, supremely, my Testament.'

You see my point? We can dispense with the body. It is very hard for us to believe that, and it was very hard for the Apostles, and that was one of the things which Jesus had to teach them in those forty days. He came and He went. The intervals between his visits grew longer, and then He left them, in His bodily presence, for ever. But not before they had learnt that lesson: that fellowship is independent of the physical form.

Learn that lesson again in these days between the Resurrection and the Ascension. When the cloud received Him out of their sight, the Apostles knew quite definitely that that could make no difference to them; that He was close to them though unseen: that when He said, 'Lo, I am with you always, even unto the end of the world,' that was plainly true, and true for evermore.

Symbols help us sometimes to realize His nearness.

Do you remember the name of Dr R. F. Horton, the eminent Minister of Lyndhurst Road Church in Hampstead for half a century. There was something of the saint in R. F. Horton. His people loved him, but they said: 'You could never *give* him anything.' Whenever their love expressed itself in a gift, he gave it at once to Overseas Missions.

So they tried again. 'We want to give you something,' they said, 'but please don't give it this time to Overseas Missions.' He promised to think and pray about it.

The guidance came. He told the somewhat disappointed deacons that in his travels round the country he had found many earnest but lonely ministers and he would like his church to do something for them.

'Let us invite them for three or four days into retreat at Lyndhurst Road,' he said. 'You can pay their fares and our people will entertain them and, under the blessing of God, they will go back to their work refreshed and eager again.'

And so it was done! It wasn't quite the personal gift the church wanted, but what can you do with a saint? When the ministers gathered from all over the country, Horton was asked to take the chair, but he begged them to leave the chair apparently empty.

'I want our Lord to preside over us,' he said. 'I will sit at His side and say such things as need saying, but let Him take the chair.'

Dr J. H. Jowett, who tells the story, said: 'It sounds nothing, but the effect of the moment was almost overwhelming, and if, at any of the meetings, any man were tempted to let fall any word that was unworthy, the sight of the empty chair froze the word upon his lips, so that it could not get itself said.'

Symbols help us sometimes to realize the unseen Presence. Use them if they do but, whether you do or not, learn again at this season of the Church year what the Apostles learned—that fellowship is *not dependent* on a body.

11

He Mounts in Triumph

Acts 1⁹—A cloud received him out of their sight

THE FOUR major festivals of the Christian Church
from earliest times were Christmas, Easter, Whitsun,
and Ascension. For centuries they were held in equal
honour throughout Christendom. Christmas and Easter
still keep their supremacy, and Whitsuntide also—though
to a less degree. It is Ascension Day which has fallen
into wide neglect.

The reasons are probably these. It is no longer a public
holiday. At one period the House of Commons adjourned
on Ascension Day, but the time came when they decided
to work on this holy festival and give themselves a holiday,
instead, on Derby Day—which, I suppose, is a parable!

Not only is it no longer a public holiday. It falls always
on a Thursday and does not receive the same stress as
Easter and Pentecost in Sunday preaching.

Moreover, it seems to some modern minds to belong
to the pre-scientific age of a flat earth, and heaven 'just
up there'. Bit by bit the festival became neglected.
People missed its spiritual heart. They could hardly see
what truth it added to the truth of the Resurrection, and
some felt that it was overshadowed by Pentecost. The
time has come when this once-great festival is barely
noticed by the mass of people in a nominally Christian
land.

It is Ascensiontide again. I want to bring home to you
once more the significance of the feast.

The head that once was crowned with thorns
  Is crowned with glory now;
A royal diadem adorns
  The mighty Victor's brow.

Let me mention some of the things which Ascension-tide means to me.

I

First, I exult in the thought that *our Lord was not taken away from us.* I stress the word 'away'. Some people seem to suppose that that is the whole meaning of the day; that now, for ever, He forsook the earth; that He retired from this plane completely until He returns in royal state. But I insist that that is not the teaching of the New Testament. Our Lord was not taken *away* from us. It is true that 'a cloud received Him out of their sight', but the cloud could not shut them out of *His* sight, and there is no reason for believing that He had gone far away.

Indeed, there is every reason for believing the opposite. For ever and ever He is wonderfully near. He said Himself, 'Lo, I am with you always, even unto the end of the world.' That means you and me. That means my friends in India and your friends in South America. The Ascension does not mean that He was taken away from us; it is just a veil which hides Him from our sight.

Most educated believers today, I find, are thinking of the Ascension in terms of the 'fourth dimension'. Rejecting—as they must—the old astronomy, and heaven localized behind that cloud above, they have thought rather of our Lord as being in the 'fourth dimension'.

But try to explain the fourth dimension to a simple man! You can't! Men who are not simple find it hard to understand. How could Palestinian peasants who first heard the gospel be expected to understand it? After twenty centuries I doubt if any of us could describe what happened with more accuracy and simplicity than this simple phrase in the Scriptures: 'A cloud received Him out of their sight.'

But he was not taken away from them. One of their great lessons—as we learned when we lingered with them in the forty days—was that fellowship was possible with Him though His human form was hid from their view.

The early disciples realized that our Lord, in going permanently into the world unseen, *had not gone away from them*. When their great High Priest passed into the heavens, they did not understand that to mean that He had passed into remoteness. The world unseen was near them: so near that He could see them all the time and hear whatever they said.

What made them sure of that?

Why, among other things, something which happened on Easter Day itself, and which occurred more than once, I imagine, through all the forty days when He was moving freely from the seen to the unseen.

Do you remember when those ten men were waiting in that locked room late on the evening of Easter Day. Presently there came a sharp tap on the door. One of them opened it, and Thomas walked in.

I think Thomas was struck immediately by their appearance. They were no longer looking hangdog and fearful, but men thrilling with a great confidence, and as he stared incredulously at them, they cried together: 'Thomas, you should have been here. The Lord has been here: been speaking with us. Thomas, He is alive.'

Thomas didn't believe a word they said. More than once, he had found himself the odd one in the Apostolic band. He felt it again now. They were more like women than men. They were afraid to face the ugly truth. Their

Lord had been murdered. He was dead. Dead men don't live again. It was all over and they had all played the coward at the last. He, at least, wasn't going to be deluded by his hopes, or feed himself on hallucinations. Almost curtly he turned from them and said: 'Except I shall see in his hands the print of the nails, and put my finger into the print of the nails, and put my hand into his side, I will not believe.'

And for a whole week they lived like that. A whole week; the ten of them saying: 'We *did* see him, Thomas'— though possibly they began to wonder themselves if there was such a thing as mass-hallucination—and Thomas defiantly replying: 'I don't believe you. Except I shall see in his hands the print of the nails . . .'

And then the eighth day came and all the eleven were in that same Upper Room once more, and suddenly the Lord was in the midst.

'Peace be unto you,' He said. (That was the local way of saying 'Good evening'.) 'Peace be unto you.'

And then, with what I imagine was something of a smile, Christ turned to Thomas and said: 'Reach hither thy finger, and see my hands; and reach hither thy hand, and put it into my side: and be not faithless, but believing.'

Now look! Those were Thomas's very words. That was what struck the dear doubter almost dumb. He had said that *very* thing. He stared at Jesus, and Jesus read in his eye all that was in his heart.

'You heard me say it, Lord? You *overheard* me. Where were you? In the world unseen? Is it as near as that? Can you both see and hear from that world unseen?' . . .

Then down on his knees goes Thomas, convinced now. 'My Lord and my God,' he cries.

Never feel superior to Thomas. I have always been grateful to him for his doubts. It would have been easy to believe that overwrought men like the disciples had imagined things, had not the appearances been so numerous and had not the disciples included a man like Thomas who found faith hard.

Grasp the truth of it. That unseen world; that world which you, in this scientific age, might prefer to think of in fourth-dimensional terms rather than 'just up there'; that world, as the Scriptures make so clear, is not a *remote* world, but those who dwell in it are very near us; as near as Thomas realized when he heard his own words quoted back to him again.

And so, through the forty days (as we saw), our Lord taught them how near it was: said to them, in effect: 'Though you cannot see me, I can see you . . .' and when Ascension Day came and the cloud received Him out of their sight, they knew, all of them, that no cloud could keep them out of *His* sight.

North, south, east, and west they went, and they all knew, in their separateness, that He was with them every one. The thinnest of veils, they now knew, hid the seen world from the unseen, and sometimes even that veil was drawn aside.

Do you remember when Stephen made his defence before the Sanhedrin, and brought down upon himself (what he must have known from the start) the capital punishment; do you remember just before they dragged him out to stone him to death, he said, 'Behold, I see the heavens opened and the Son of man standing on the right hand of God'? The veil was drawn aside for Stephen.

Do you remember, when Peter was on the roof-top at Joppa, and had to make that major decision concerning the admission of the Gentiles into the Christian Church; do you remember that the veil was drawn aside then, and how he was counselled from Heaven what he had to do?

And do you remember, also, that when Paul hurtled

along the Damascus road and came to his great meeting, how again the veil was drawn aside and the effulgent light of the unseen world streamed into this, and a light above the brightness of the sun blinded the Apostle, but made him to see, even in his blindness, with whom he was dealing, and made him to hear the voice like the sound of many waters: 'I am Jesus whom thou persecutest . . .'?

Grasp it! The unseen world is very near the seen world. The cloud hides Him from your sight, but He has not removed into some far-off realm of being.

'Still He loves the earth He leaves.'

II

Here is the *second* thing I exult in at Ascensiontide: *our humanity is now in highest heaven.*

> *And didst Thou love the race that loved not Thee*
> *And didst Thou take to heaven a* human *brow . . .*

A *human* brow!

> *By that one likeness which is ours and Thine*
> *By that one nature which doth hold us kin.*

One nature! *Kin!*

I have heard theologians talk at times about the impassivity of God; 'God can't *feel*,' they had said. How can the Supreme Being of the Universe be troubled by our trifling and transient pangs?

I might have believed them had I not seen God, in Jesus, suffering on the Cross, and might even have had my own sufferings multiplied by the belief that I suffered without understanding or compassion from above.

I spurn it as a libel on the character of God. Incarnation added even to the experience of God. The author of the Epistle to the Hebrews said that our Lord *learned* things by His sufferings.

And how much of suffering He had! The scheming plots of His enemies. The misunderstanding of His friends. The torturing slowness of His passion at times. (Remember His word to Judas: 'What thou doest, do quickly.' Get it over!) The blood of the garden and the pillar and the Cross . . .

All in highest heaven now! Our humanity in heaven! Scars in heaven! I exult in it!

> *The dear tokens of His passion*
> Still *His dazzling body bears*.

I am told that scientists have an instrument called a spectroscope by which they are able to study the chemistry of the other planets. By means of the spectroscope they assert that there is *one* chemistry of the heavenly bodies: that oxygen is oxygen on Venus, and nitrogen is still nitrogen on Mars.

I see a parable in that. Pure love is pure love in heaven and on earth as well. The virtues God nurtures on earth are found in their fullness above. This world and *that* world are not unrelated and each incomprehensible to the other.

> *One family we dwell in Him,*
> *One Church, above, beneath*.

And that is true, most of all, because He bridged the gulf and carried our humanity back into Glory. He understands that our sufferings and our noblest sacrifices are but a faint reflection of His own.

Do you know the name of Rabbi Bluoch? He was a Jewish padre in the French Army in the first World War. Men of the Jewish faith in the French Army are naturally not numerous and the Padre's chance of finding one whenever he went out into no-man's-land was slight. Far the larger number of dying men were Roman Catholics.

The Rabbi, therefore, always carried a crucifix with him to comfort any sinking Christian he might find. It was, indeed, as he was holding the crucifix before the eyes of a dying soldier that the fatal bullet came and drilled the Rabbi through.

What an argument some doctrinaires would make of that! 'But he wasn't a Christian himself . . . ! What could a crucifix mean to him . . . ? What would other Jews think . . . ?'

Let them argue! It was love, compassion, magnanimity . . . It was all understood by our ascended Lord. Our true sacrifices reflect His own.

Our humanity is in heaven.

One nature holds us kin.

III

Here is the *third* thing in which I exult at this season. *The Ascension is the most emphatic sign of Victory.* He has conquered. The golden gates are lifted up and the King goes in to His throne.

> *See the Conqueror mounts in triumph*
> *See the King in royal state . . .*

Have you noticed in your study of the Scriptures that the seers and the apostles in their times of deepest perplexity and decision were often sustained by a vision of the heavenly throne. In the year that King Uzziah died (and of his own great dedication) Isaiah saw the Lord 'sitting upon the throne!' When Ezekiel was sustaining the forlorn remnant of exiles, he saw the throne. When Daniel discussed 'the abomination of desolation' he saw the throne. When St John was exiled on Patmos and had his great vision, he saw the throne.

Why the throne?—God's throne?

To reassure them whose universe it is. A monarch reigns from a throne. It is the symbol of authority. Jesus ascends to the throne.

The suffering dying Jesus is the Christ upon the throne.

It is *His* world. All authority has been given unto Him. Exult at this Ascensiontide as you see Him take the throne.

> *Hark those bursts of acclamation;*
> *Hark, those loud triumphant chords:*
> *Jesus takes the highest station:*
> *O what joy the sight affords!*
> *Crown Him! Crown Him!*
> *King of kings, and Lord of lords.*

I know quite well that this world doesn't look as though it belongs to Jesus. Murder, lust, rape, greed, selfishness, pride and jealousy are spread wide across it, and the battle between good and evil seems as sharp as it ever was.

But the real victory is already won. Christ overcame the world at Calvary. 'Be of good cheer,' He said. 'I have overcome the world.' Unconvincing though appearances may be, it is *His* world now. He is on the throne.

Fighting goes on long after a campaign is lost. Napoleon's hopes of world conquest really ended in 1805 at Trafalgar. He didn't give up till 1815 at Waterloo. Some people think the Germans lost the last war in September 1940 at the Battle of Britain. It was never in serious dispute after El Alamein and Stalingrad. But there was much bitter fighting still to endure.

Grim though the appearances are, the devil has lost on this planet. Christ is King! See Him on the throne! At this season of Ascension, crown Him again in your hearts.

Crown the Saviour, angels crown Him;
Rich the trophies Jesus brings:
In the seat of power enthrone Him
While the vault of heaven rings.
Crown Him! Crown Him!
Crown the Saviour, King of kings.

IV

Here is the final ground of my rejoicing in the Ascension, the last, at least, I will mention today. It reminds us again that *on the other side of death is a known and dear Friend.*

Don't let's pretend! We all fear death in some way. At least we have an *awe* of it—and that by God's design.

If we had no awe of death, suicide would be more common than it is. Any sharp pain, or disappointment, or fright, would lead us to take this easy way out. So God, in love, set a sentinel at the gate and no sane person can think of his own death without awe . . . or some without dread.

What helps us to overcome the dread? The knowledge that on the other side of death is a known and dear Friend.

I once visited the Hawaiian Islands and found them almost as lovely as the tourist agencies said they were. What perfect weather they enjoy! Even the rain is called 'liquid sunshine'. As I walked on a beach near Honolulu in the rays of the setting sun one evening, I remembered a story I had heard.

An English lad of eleven lost both parents in a motor accident and resolved to go to Honolulu. He knew of its lovely climate, but it wasn't that which pulled him across a wide ocean, a wide continent and half another ocean as well. Indeed, he dreaded the journey. 'Will my tickets be in order? How much do I tip the steward on the boat? What happens if I'm stranded in New York or San Francisco? . . .' With all these fears churning inside him, people who didn't know wondered why he was so resolute to make the journey.

'Oh?' he said. 'Don't you know? My elder brother is there.'

Not chiefly for the palms, the weather, or the songs but . . . 'my elder brother is there'.

I share your awe of death. I clutch at earth too, but the awe isn't dread and there are times when the prospect is thrilling. *My Elder Brother is there.*

Ascensiontide reminds me of it again and that is another reason why I love this season of the year.

12

He 'Pours Forth' The Spirit

Acts 2³³—*Being therefore by the right hand of God exalted, and having received of the Father the promise of the Holy Ghost, he hath poured forth this . . .*

WE HAVE come to the day of Pentecost and, therefore, to the birthday of the Church, for the Church was born when the Holy Spirit was given.

We are told in our text that when Jesus was exalted, He 'poured forth' the Holy Spirit and it is of a special part of the work of the Holy Spirit that I want to speak now.

The Holy Spirit is referred to in the New Testament by various terms and, among others, by the term 'paraclete'. The word 'paraclete' comes from two simple Greek words: *para*, which (in this connexion) means 'alongside', and *kaleo*, which means 'to call' or 'to summon'. The word is usually employed in the context of a court of law. So you get the picture: one 'called alongside of', and the word is sometimes translated 'comforter', and sometimes 'counsellor', but best of all it is translated 'advocate'.

In legal English the word means 'barrister'. They seldom use the word 'barrister' in Scotland. For the same office they use the better term 'advocate', and it is with the Holy Spirit as an Advocate that I am concerned now.

The function of an advocate at any time is to *plead*. It is an office of distinction. If some girl you knew were going to marry a barrister (or advocate) you—because, like most other people, you may have a way of assessing people not at their real worth, but by the kind of work they do—would be disposed to think that she was marrying well.

There is, of course, a professional code operative with advocates. It has two chief principles. Just as there is a bond of absolute secrecy between a minister and the members of his flock when they come to speak of their spiritual needs or confess their sins; just as there is a bond of absolute secrecy between a doctor and his patient in all that concerns the patient's health; so the relationship between the advocate and his client is absolutely confidential too. Not even a court of law can compel the disclosure of any communication which takes place between them. The prisoner can speak his whole mind to his advocate, and the advocate will hold it in absolute confidence.

And the other great duty of an advocate is that he must do his best for his client at all costs. It may be that, in his private conversations with the man he is representing, admissions are made or hints are given which leave the advocate uncertain as to his client's integrity. Indeed, his piercing brain might even conclude that, on terms of strict justice, there isn't much to be said for the man. Nevertheless, his professional calling and his advocate's honour require that he does his best for him; his *very* best.

Carry that truth over to the high office of the Holy Spirit as Advocate, for in the New Testament that is one of His exalted names.

I

Notice, first, that He is an Advocate when He pleads *WITH* us

> *Christ is our Advocate on high;*
> *Thou art our Advocate within:*
> *O plead the truth, and make reply*
> *To every argument of sin.*

The arguments of sin? What does that mean?

The psychologist (with his love of awkward phrases) calls it 'the rationalization of desire'. What does he mean by that? I can tell you.

Maybe next Sunday, when it is time for worship, you will look out of the window and find that it is a beautiful day, and you begin to think like this:

'Of course, it is right to go to worship. I have a duty to my soul and to God. But, then, I have a duty to my body as well, and I have been cramped up in the office all the week. What I really need is a change of air.

'Yes, and, moreover, there is old Bill down at the coast. Now, Bill must be very depressed having a holiday on his own with no one to cheer him up. Surely it is my duty as a friend to go down and see dear old Bill?

'And, of course, I need not neglect my soul entirely. I can read some nice, improving book in the train or take it with me in the car. That will probably do me more good than being in church. . . .'

You see how it runs? That is what the psychologist calls 'the rationalization of desire', and that is what the hymn-writer had in mind when he spoke of 'the arguments of sin'.

David knew it.

I think it would be difficult to get into little space all the evil which David crowded into the great sin of his life. He wanted the wife of one of his officers. He saw her and saw that she was beautiful. While his army was on active service fighting the King's battles, David seduced the woman. Then, fearing the consequences, he 'arranged' the death of her husband and added murder to royal lust. The man after God's own heart wallowed in sin!

How did he ever get there?

This way. By the rationalization of desire. By the arguments of sin.

H

This is how it happened. A sinful thought crossed his mind, and this he could not help. But he dwelt on it when he should have blacked it out. He fed his imagination on it when he should have killed it with a prayer. He told himself that Uriah, the woman's husband, had died in the discharge of his duty. Gallant soldiers do fall, of course, on the field of battle . . .! And then he married the woman and that, of course, as any lying adulterer knows, is supposed to rub the adultery out. He was a victim of the arguments of sin.

Look at me in the face and tell me: do you know anything about the arguments of sin?

Something tells me that you do.

Tell me this also: when, in the court of your soul, evil desire began to plead the arguments of sin, was there no other voice in that court pleading for *noble* things? Wasn't there a voice, low but clear and insistent, speaking to you of the best that you had ever been taught at home, in church, by your good mother; pleading, pleading like a skilful advocate in front of a judge, bringing up every good point from the past which will help his case? . . Do you remember that in your own soul? Who was it? I'll tell you who it was. It was the blessed Paraclete. It was the Holy Spirit. He was pleading the truth and making reply to every argument of sin.

Where would *I* have been, where would *you* have been, but for that blessed Paraclete? If, at our first foolish fingering of sin; if, as soon as we were seduced in our hearts by desire; if, when our vagrant wishes ran after that suggestive image; if He had left us without a word . . . where should we have been?

If you are strong in virtue; if there is at least a little bit of your soul defended against the assaults of passion; if there is something saved still from the inroads of worldliness . . . it is all the work of the blessed Paraclete.

And listen! *He is always there.* You may grieve Him, and turn a deaf ear to Him, and by not heeding Him, the voice may grow faint, but I don't believe He has left (*entirely* left!) any one of you.

Did you see the report of that case in the courts the other day? A member of the Bar had to plead 'invisibility' at the Sheffield Quarter Sessions because he was not wearing his wig and gown. That is one of the rules of our courts. Officially he is not present. There was a prisoner in the dock, and he wanted the barrister to plead for him, but the Judge said that he could not see the barrister because, according to our laws, the Judge can only see an advocate when he is properly attired.

What a position for the poor prisoner! Dumb in the presence of undeniable guilt. No one to plead for him. No one to say: 'My Lord, think on the extenuating circumstances.' No one to say: 'He has a good record; he didn't mean to do it.'

The Holy Spirit will never desert you. You can drive Him away, but He will go unwillingly. He wants to plead with you. He knows the worst about you and He longs to save.

I am bold to say that there is not one of you here present tonight (whether you have accepted the offer of God in Christ or not), who, by the mercy of God, doesn't know something in your conscience of the work of the Holy Spirit as Advocate. He has pleaded *with* you!

II

Not only does He plead with us; He pleads *IN* us.

I mean this. Put quite simply, prayer is the heart of our religion. That is the fact of it. People say to me sometimes: 'I am no theologian or philosopher. Put it simply to me, preacher. What is the real heart of this Christian religion? How do you grow in what you call "grace and power" . . .?'

Prayer is the heart of it.

I know that many of our ideas are confused concerning prayer. I know that people pray for things that can only come by work, and sometimes work for things that can only come by prayer.

A woman once told me that she was leaving the church and never coming back again, and when I asked her why, she said that her little girl had sat for a scholarship and, as her mother, she had prayed hard that her little girl would pass. She not only had *not* passed, but she was at the bottom of the list! So that proved there was nothing in prayer, and she was not coming to church any more.

The folly of it! It doesn't look as though I had taught *her* much about prayer. I take the blame upon myself.

I knew her little girl. She couldn't have won a scholarship for love or money. She hadn't got the brains for that.

She was a charming girl; she will be grown up now; she is probably the 'queen' of some nice home and making her man happy. But a scholarship!—not on your life.

Yet think of her mother losing faith in prayer because of that.

And there are other people who only pray when they are in extremity. They look upon prayer as a strong drug which you only turn to when you are in urgent danger, like the man not used to the ways of churches on whom a minister called because he had heard that the man was ill.

When the minister was ready to go he said a little tentatively to the sick man: 'Shall I offer a word of prayer before I go?'

And the pale fellow in the bed turned paler still and said:

'O! no, thank you; I'm not as bad as that.'

What would you think of a friend who only turned up when he wanted something? But that is how a good many of us treat God. We ignore Him until we want something desperately for ourselves and then we pray.

All this proves that people's thought about prayer is muddled. But listen! Even when our thought about prayer is *clear*, what awful sloth we have in it. God forgive us, though prayer is the heart of our religion, what poor craftsmen most of us are at praying.

Did you ever spend sixpence on a book of 'helps' to prayer? Did you ever stay up late—no, not to finish your novel—but to pray? Did you ever rise early—no, not just to start on an excursion, but to pray?

Now, here is our dilemma as I see it; our Christian dilemma. Our growth in Christ depends upon prayer . . . and yet we cannot pray. Not really! The *longing* to pray is not in us. We have to *push* ourselves to our knees. What a plight! The very thing we most need, we have such little desire for.

How can we escape from this impasse?

Go to God! Tell God the dilemma that you are in. Tell Him frankly. Tell him you know you will never grow in spiritual things without prayer and tell Him honestly, as you must, that you have no real appetite for it.

And listen—I'll tell you what He will do. He will do for you what our Monarch in England would do for any poor wretch who was in a similar plight; He will provide you Himself with a counsel. He will!

The law of Britain will not allow any man to stand accused in a court of law without a professional advocate to plead his case. If the accused is unable to provide the advocate himself, the Crown assumes the responsibility.

And the King of Heaven will do more than that for

you. He will provide you, not a King's or Queen's Counsel, but the King of Kings' Counsel: the Paraclete; the Advocate; the blessed Holy Spirit. He will plead *in* you. He will put in you a passion, a flame of prayer. 'The Spirit also helpeth our infirmities, for we know not how to pray as we ought.' With passing time He may even give you the gift of *infused* prayer. You will know that you are being *prayed through*.

I do not say that this will happen every day. There may *still* be times when you must prod yourself to prayer, but I *do* say that increasingly the desire to pray will possess you and that, as you pray, your sense of power in prayer will so increase that your busiest day will seem a day ill-spent unless it has included some time given to prayer.

And that is the second great task of the Holy Spirit as Advocate; He pleads *in* us.

III

And notice finally that He pleads *THROUGH* us. *With* us, and *in* us, and *through* us. He pleads through us to the world of men.

It says in the New Testament that one of the functions of the Advocate is to convict the world of sin. What need there is of that!

It is one of the tragedies of the times that there is no acute sense of sin. People do the most awful things and think nothing of it. They are guilty of the most ghastly unfaithfulness to their marriage vows; they take things that do not belong to them; to lie and hate and smear people seems, in many quarters, no longer to be wrong; it is only wrong to be found out.

O! that the Holy Spirit would plead *through* us and convict the world of sin.

Think of the folly of war! Are we free of war even yet? Will it never come back again? Are you sure?

You are *not* sure! The world is not yet convicted of the sin and insanity of war.

Or think of the widespread sin of pride. How men boast of things which are really gifts of God! Think of the intellectual snobbery—as though they gave themselves their brains. Or they boast of their birth—as though they chose their parents. What forms of foolish pride we witness day after day! But can you convince them of it?

I do not know. The very effort to do it on our own seems to label us as 'prigs'. I think only the Holy Spirit can do it. O! that He would plead through us, and convict the world of sin.

Let us ask Him to do it. He will begin by first pointing out to us, with loving firmness, the sins which still survive in our own souls, and then plead through us—by our lives more than our words—to make sin self-conscious in those with whom we come in contact.

I am a preacher but in nothing do I fail more completely in my preaching than in convicting people of sin. I come here week by week and, like some poor, stammering advocate, plead the case for my Lord. Yet I do not know how to convict people of sin. My words are not enough. I need something more than a ready tongue . . . I need the power of the Holy Spirit.

Nor is this a need of preachers only: *you* need it too.

Maybe you are working with people, and living with people, deep in sin and unaware of it; oozing self-satisfaction; strutting about and saying 'What's the matter with *me?*'

How will you convince them?

You can't! Not alone! You need the Holy Spirit to plead *through* you.

Saviour, it is the Day of Pentecost. Pour forth the Divine Advocate into all our needy hearts that He may plead *with* us, and *in* us, and *through* us. For Thy name's sake. Amen.

13

He Shares Society in the Godhead

Matthew 28¹⁹—*In the name of the Father, and of the Son,
and of the Holy Ghost.* . . .

I REMEMBER, many years ago, following three
children out of morning worship from a Sussex village
chapel. It was Trinity Sunday. The girl was aged about
fourteen and the boys about twelve and ten.

The elder boy said to his sister: 'I can't understand all
this "three in one and one in three" business.'

'I can't understand it either,' she said, 'but I think of it
this way. Mother is "Mumma" to us; she is "Mabel" to
Daddy, and she is "Mrs Douglas" to lots of other
people. . . .'

Is that the answer then? Is it just a question of names?
Are we right in finding the doctrine of the Trinity in this
text because 'name' is singular, and the names themselves
(Father, Son and Holy Ghost) are plural'.

No! It is deeper than that—adroit as the little girl was
in finding an analogy which could help her through childhood. The doctrine of the Holy Trinity is nowhere mentioned under that term in Scripture—though the doctrine
is clearly there by implication. We have come to the
central mystery of the Christian faith and we may as well
settle with ourselves as we begin this sermon that we shall
not *fully* understand the mystery at the end.

Not that that need depress us unduly! It is commonly
agreed among all who believe in God that 'a God com-
prehended is no God'. *Could* a Being fully understood by
mortals be God? We should expect—not the irrational,

certainly—but just as certainly, the unfathomable; a deep where all our thoughts are drowned. But let us venture forward! It is Trinity Sunday again, the only great day in the Christian year not associated with an event, but purely with doctrine. Yet what doctrine!—rooted in experience, beaten out on the anvil of the Church's early life, defined, not to make things hard for plain men, but to have all the elements in place for the growing comprehension as it comes; the highest, holiest mystery to which mortals can aspire. The Church Fathers knew better than we do how superficially absurd it would seem. 'Three in One, and One in Three.' What a field for the thin humour of those who are ready to engineer a joke out of blasphemy! But a field also for those ready to remove their shoes on holy ground and—in speechless adoration—to be lost in wonder, love and praise.

We live in an age when the fashionable philosophy puts much stress on logic and denies the usefulness of any discussion not conducted in terms precisely defined. And what an impregnable position that is!—even if it does kill much discussion on most of the fascinating mysteries of life. The Doctrine of the Trinity, these philosophers assert, is not discussible. 'To ask us', they say, 'whether it is true or false is silly; the terms you use are meaningless. It is, indeed, what the average man already suspects, just "playing with words".'

All right! Let us see! We are average men and women. We have our Bibles under our hand (as it were) and our intelligence alert. How came the Church to believe that the highest mystery of all Life is a Tri-Unity: that the Godhead is ONE in *three*, and THREE in *one*?

I

God—the Creator

The Bible opens with the words, 'In the beginning

God . . .'. So—when the record was set down—man already had clear concepts. He could say 'God'.

We do not know in full detail the whole religious history of our race. Travellers have found primitive people with only the haziest idea of a supreme God (and sometimes not even that), but living in what they believe to be a world much influenced by spirits—kind and unkind too. When men came to the idea of gods, the gods were many, and sometimes tied to the tribe and sometimes tied to the soil. Israel had Jehovah, but the Moabites had Chemosh. When Naaman, the cleansed leper, returned to Syria, he did so feeling that he must still pay his respects to the local god, to Rimmon, but he took some soil of Israel with him on which to offer worship to Jehovah, to whom he now felt he owed his health.

The penetrating awareness that there is but One Living God of the whole world is the glory of the Hebrew people, and the reason why they rank with Greece and Rome as teachers of humanity. One God—for all. Only one! 'Hear, O Israel, the Lord our God is one'—and all other 'gods' are 'fabled deities'. As they came to perceive the nature of the Universal God as holy, just, merciful, loving . . . they gained an awareness of God which was later to be filled out and gloriously enriched, but true in all these amazing insights. No wonder an historian, comparing the Hebrews to the other tribes which lived beside them centuries before Christ in the Near East, said that the Hebrews appeared as sober men in a world of drunkards. One God! The Creator and Sustainer of all that is. How childish even Greek and Roman mythology seem beside this! Warring gods! Deities guilty of conduct a mortal conscience would condemn. *This* is the truth! One God! Holy, just, merciful, loving. . . . If this be true, would anything else matter much or matter long?—war? pain? parting? bereavement? No! None of them *ultimately*—if God is like that and everything is in His loving hands.

Other people have come to the conviction of One Supreme God, not so much by revelation as by reflection. They have looked at the world, seen its mixed character (lovely sunsets and hideous earthquakes; little lambs and vipers; mother love and rotting disease) and, while they couldn't deny the contradictions, they have concluded that the world had One Creator who was good. 'The grain of things runs to goodness,' they have said. 'I was *made* that way. Something dreadful mars it now, but the foul is an alien and intrusive element. The original design was beneficent. The ground-plan of creation is good. It has but one Maker and He is kind.'

Some thinkers, it is true, have believed that the elements of good and evil behind the universe are equally mighty and all life is an expression of their conflict, but this view has not prevailed in the history of thought. More and more of those who believe in God—some by revelation and some by reflection though most by both—have been convinced that there is One Great Being behind this universe; variously named it is true, the Prime Cause, the Absolute, the God of Abraham, Isaac and Jacob . . . ONE, the Creator and Sustainer of all existence and the true Object of all praise.

Historically, as we have seen, the people of Israel were the most perceptive of God and of His character; they grasped the truth of God's identity, unity and nature, while their neighbours believed in a multiplicity of 'gods' and made them of wood and stone. Moreover, they built this knowledge of God into the very structure of their children's minds and made them aware of God's unity from their tenderest years.

In this faith, the fishermen of Galilee were brought up and were holding their faith with resolute firmness when an amazing experience befell them in the third decade of what we now call the Christian era.

Let us seek to share that experience with them.

II

God—the Redeemer

He came from Nazareth and was called Jesus. The fishermen of Capernaum noticed nothing peculiar about His dress or His accent, but His words, and His power, and the impress of His whole personality were almost beyond belief. He was a carpenter by trade and had had no more formal schooling than they had had themselves, but 'never man so spake'. He held the lake-shore crowds in the hollow of His hands and spoke with such authority that He compelled them to hear.

He had supernatural powers too. He could heal the sick with a touch or a word. On His first Sabbath in Capernaum, He seemed to be healing all day, and others besides the fishermen felt that the Kingdom of Heaven had come. When He said to some of these men who earned their living in boats, 'Follow me,' they couldn't resist Him. Though they had duties to their parents and one, at least, was a married man, 'they forsook all and followed him'.

Altogether, He chose twelve companions and they lived closely with Him for two or three years; saw Him at all hours of day and night; when He was tired and hungry, and influential people were scheming to have Him murdered; when He was on the crest of the wave and thousands were wanting to make Him King. . . . He never became small, petty, revengeful, personally ambitious. . . . Indeed, wonderful as He seemed to them at the beginning, He seemed more wonderful with passing time. He was strangely different from anyone else they had ever known.

Women were not 'chattels' to Him—nor even as inferior as their own law allowed. He could keep company with notorious evil-doers and remain unstained. The winds obeyed Him, and mental disease defeated Him as little as physical. Three of them once saw Him positively transfigured and overheard Him in conversation with people from another plane of being. The mystery of His nature deepened for His adoring companions and the conviction grew in them that He was the Christ, the Messiah, the promised deliverer of their people. Precisely who or what the Messiah would be not even the leaders of Israel had clearly defined, nor did these fishermen pause (it seems) to ponder. 'This is He,' they said, and one day Peter spoke it aloud in the face of their Master. 'Thou art the Christ', he said, 'the Son of the Living God.'

Yet not even this high imprecision could satisfy them all the days of their life.

They noticed other things.

He accepted worship *as His right*. Worship is for God alone.

He forgave sins and (as the scribes so justly remarked) 'Who can forgive sins, but God only?'

He had no sense of personal sin—a phenomenon quite unknown among truly good men—and He said such things about Himself as labelled Him either as mad or . . . (but how can a Jew say it?) God Himself. 'He that hath seen me hath seen the Father.' 'I am the bread of life.' 'Before Abraham was, I am.' 'I and the Father are one.'

But they brushed that aside while He was with them. To be sure that He was the Messiah come to vindicate Israel was enough. They followed Him on Palm Sunday in triumph into Jerusalem like His pre-selected cabinet, and when it all crashed in Gethsemane they ran for it and the only one of them left there was the traitor who kissed Him into His murderers' arms.

Fuller understanding came only after the Resurrection. To all the incredibilities of His life this crowning in-credibility was added. He rose again from the dead. They saw, and saw, and saw Him again. Through forty days! Oddly enough, it was Thomas who first realized more than the rest all that this meant. Jesus was not a mortal adopted to Messiahship. He was God incarnate here on earth. Said Thomas: 'My Lord and *my God!*' The disciples were Jews to a man—and devout—but they were now sure of this. God had visited and redeemed His people. 'Hear O Israel the Lord our God is one'—but God was not only Sovereign but Saviour; not only Creator but Redeemer; not only *above* us but *among* us. Did Thomas mean by 'God' all that we mean? Who can say? He said it—and the implications worked themselves out.

Years before the Gospels were written, Paul was writing the mind of all the Apostles concerning Jesus. Christ 'counted it not a prize to be on an equality with God'; 'Christ . . . who is over all, God blessed for ever'. Paul speaks of 'the grace of God and of the Lord Jesus Christ' and 'looking for the blessed hope and appearing of the glory of our great God and Saviour Jesus Christ'.

So these devout men came to realize that there is society in the Godhead and—after Pentecost—they realized also that it wasn't limited to the Father and the Son.

III

God—the Sanctifier

During the last solemn talks Jesus had with His disciples at the close of His earthly ministry, He spoke much about a Comforter, an Advocate, a Spirit of Truth who would come when He had gone. He referred to Him as a Person. 'When *he*, the Spirit of truth is come. . . .' He put so much stress upon this, and so much value, that it was tantamount to saying: 'You'll be better off when I'm gone.' 'The works that I do will you do also and *greater works than these*. . . .' That the disciples took only a limited notice of what He said about the Holy Spirit is further proof of the preoccupation of their minds in those days with more immediate things—the earthly Kingdom they believed Him to be founding. They took as little heed of the announcement of His impending death and rising again. But, after the Resurrection and His further reminders, it took a foremost place in their mind and after the Ascension they thought of little else. Absorbed in prayer together, they awaited the coming of the Holy Spirit.

He came at Pentecost. Wonders attended His coming hard to describe in human speech—and tongues of fire and some strange gift of communication which overleapt the barriers of normal language. But the precious and abiding truth was that God was now *in* them and they could part from one another while God stayed with them all.

Even when Jesus was with them in the flesh, He couldn't be in two places at once. Lazarus could die, his weeping sisters beside him, but Jesus wasn't there.

Moreover, the disciples had come to realize that in the quest of holiness, it wasn't enough to have God *near* you. Christ could be only a couple of paces away and they could quarrel with one another about who would be greatest when His Kingdom came, elbowing for a good place when He was almost in the shadow of the Cross! They needed help nearer than *near*. If they were to have victory over the sin and selfishness inside them, they must have God *inside* them too, remaking their nature, beating the evil down, and making divine love the motive of all they did.

Slowly, the awareness of what had happened grew upon them in the days succeeding Pentecost. The Saviour had fulfilled His word. The Holy Spirit was within them —to make them holy too; to impart His own fruit (love, joy, peace, patience, kindness, goodness, faithfulness, humility and self-control); to convict the world of sin through them and make them mighty in evangelism.

So—to evangelism they went. No dependable record survives of their travels. Did Thomas get to India, as some believe? Did all the Apostles but John die for the faith? We do not know. But wherever they went, the Holy Spirit went *in* them, breaking the sin in their nature, moulding them to holiness, pleading in prayer, exalting the Saviour, convicting the world of sin.

From the earliest years of the Church the threefold blessing was in use. The grace of the Lord Jesus Christ, the love of God, the fellowship of the Holy Spirit. . . . I say again: these men were devout Jews and never departed from the central conviction of Judaism. God is One. But One in Three, and Three in One. Creator; Redeemer; Sanctifier. The Father in majesty; the Son in suffering; the Spirit in striving.

And it was from the Church's experience that this doctrine arose. It wasn't fashioned (as some seem to suppose) to make a simple thing difficult for ordinary people. 'This is how we met God,' said the Apostles in effect, and the Church sought, as she formulated her doctrine, to put into ordered thought an experience implicit in all parts of the New Testament.

'Tis mystery all.

But life often presents us with facts of experience irreconcilable at one stage of knowledge—though better understood at another. For years astronomers could not explain the behaviour of the planet Uranus. On the then established knowledge of the solar system, Uranus *couldn't* act as it did—*yet it did!* It was quite absurd—yet it happened. 'We don't understand it,' said the astronomers, though two of them independently made a guess which proved right. When the planet Neptune was discovered, the mystery was cleared up.

Study, observation, experience, compel us as mortals in

whom knowledge slowly grows to assert at times facts not easily harmonized with one another. Yet loyalty to truth at that stage requires the seemingly absurd insistence. . . . We *can't* fully explain it, but these are facts of the mystery as we know them to be.

So the early Church came to say: 'God the Father; God the Son; God the Holy Ghost. Three Persons, but One God.' The early fathers used the word 'Person', not to limit God to our level, but because personality was the highest they knew and God could not be *less* than that. How much more? . . . Well, how could mortals say?

Three in One. God above us; God among us; God within us. God in origins; God in history; God in experience.

It is Trinity Sunday. We are at the central mystery of our most holy faith. Let us adore the Great Triune God!

14

'He has a Special Love for Little Children'

John 21¹⁵—*Feed my lambs*

I

JESUS CHRIST was vitally interested in little children; indeed, 'interest' is much too mild a term. He loved them deeply and seems never to have missed an opportunity of showing His love. Again and again, in the Gospel story, we find references to children upon His lips. He speaks of a woman's joy at the birth of her child; He mentions the readiness of parents to give good gifts to their children; He refers to a father's unwillingness to leave his bed at a late hour and so disturb his little ones; He observes the petulance of children sometimes when they are at play.

When He comes to speak of the big price He may demand of His followers in their loyalty to Him, He says it may even be necessary to leave their children—and He mentions this as one who realizes how great is the sacrifice involved.

Not only was Christ a keen observer of children—He was also their true friend. Many of His works of healing were performed upon young people. When His friends would have kept the children from His presence, He protested indignantly, and when He had taken them in His arms He blessed them with a fervency which is almost unparalleled in the Gospels.

Nor was Christ merely the observer and friend of children. The teacher in Him was attracted by them as well. He chose the childlike spirit as the true temper for all candidates who sought admittance to the Kingdom He had come to found, and He declared that the humility of the child was an essential element in all genuine greatness. He identified Himself with children in a very intimate way when He said: 'Whosoever shall receive one such little child in my name receiveth me.' He promised that the smallest service rendered to children would be repaid: 'Whosoever shall give to drink unto one of these little ones a cup of cold water only, in the name of a disciple, verily I say unto you, he shall in no wise lose his reward.'

Nor did He mince His words, or soften His expression, when He came to deal with those who would harm the child: 'Whoso shall cause one of these little ones which believe on me to stumble, it is profitable for him that a great millstone should be hanged about his neck, and that he should be sunk in the depth of the sea.'

Finally, on that great day when He stood on the shores of the lake of Gennesareth, and delivered His final behest to His repentant disciple, He said: 'Feed my lambs'— and perhaps no demand He placed upon His followers is more important than this.

II

But it is very hard, in some ways, to feed His lambs today —in the sense of giving them spiritual instruction in the faith. Their own parents often obstruct us in the doing of it. They give no real religious teaching to their children themselves, and do not send them to the Sunday-school or the Children's Church to let us do it for them. This is nominally a Christian country . . . but it is not an exaggeration to say that a generation has arisen which knows not Jesus.

During the childhood of those now in middle life

almost every child went to Sunday-school. The parents insisted. They might not attend church themselves, but they were firm that their young people should go. Their motives may have been a little shabby—it may have been their way of securing a sleep on a Sunday afternoon—but, whatever the motive, the children went. That was the important thing. Under the instruction of wise teachers, and still more under the influence of their loving hearts, children were won to discipleship.

Alas! that is no longer true. The time came when the Sunday-school was scorned. Feeble wits caricatured it as a place where 'repressed females spent their time telling Tommy to take the toffee out of his mouth and tuck his toes in' . . . and for all that scorn and neglect of Sunday school the bill is coming in. It is not quite so funny now you see what the neglect involves.

Juvenile crime is appallingly widespread. It is not confined to one social stratum.

A few years ago two boys of Wellington College in Berkshire—one of the leading public schools of our land —were sent for trial for housebreaking. With skill and with persistence, they repeatedly burgled the houses of the neighbourhood, and their ages at the time of their committal were sixteen and seventeen. Anybody with a concern for the moral well-being of England might well be appalled by the spread of juvenile crime.

In a recent youth survey in Manchester it was revealed that over 70 per cent of the youth of that northern city between the ages of fourteen and twenty-five were utterly untouched by church, Sunday-school, evening institute, voluntary organization, or wholesome club of any kind.

Still more recently we have been startled by the carefully tabulated statement of Admiral Sir Geoffrey Layton, Commander-in-Chief at Portsmouth.

He has been taking heed of the religious knowledge and

convictions of the men being called up for the Navy—young men between the ages of eighteen and nineteen—and this is what he has discovered:

Only 23 per cent could repeat the Lord's Prayer.

28 per cent knew something about it.

49 per cent—that is, nearly half—only knew the opening phrase.

72 per cent knew who Jesus Christ was, but only 39 per cent knew where He was born.

83 per cent didn't even know what Christmas Day celebrates.

62 per cent knew the meaning of Good Friday, but only 45 per cent knew what Easter was about.

As to Pentecost, the percentage fell then to 2·5 per cent. Think of that! Only one man in forty knew the meaning of Whitsun.

Strangely enough, 15 per cent claimed to have been confirmed, but, as the Admiral himself remarked—and he is devoted to the Church of England—how they could have got through their instruction for confirmation without learning about the descent of the Holy Spirit he does not know.

73 per cent put down their religion as Church of England; the rest belonged to the Free Churches and the Roman Catholic Church.

95 per cent of the Roman Catholics attended a religious service. 75 per cent of the Free Churchmen attended their Church, and were what he regarded as 'effective members'. In the Church of England, the figure fell to 20 per cent.

You will draw what conclusions you like from those solemn figures so carefully assessed, but it seems to me that you would be mistaken if you supposed that, in any serious sense of the word, England is still a Christian land.

III

Throughout my ministry I have tried to discover the reasons for the reluctance of parents to send their children to church or Sunday-school, and I want to put some of the reasons before you now.

(i) Some seem to object almost on the basis of class distinction. They seem to put Sunday-school in the same category as the old-time Ragged School, and, while they suppose that it would have value for *some* children, it would hardly have value for *theirs*. Their children didn't need it. They were growing up in a good home and under the influence of decent parents, and the assumption was that any child who grew up under their influence didn't need a Sunday-school.

I think it needs to be said plainly to parents like that, that sin can enter the heart of youth—and does enter it —at any social level. Sin is in our nature. If virtue is to be buttressed in us; if the good is to triumph; if Jesus Christ is to find an entrance into these hearts, something must be done about it, and it must be done when the children are small.

The reason why Admiral Layton can say that 95 per cent of the Roman Catholics attend a church service is to be explained by the impressions made on the minds of Roman Catholic children when they are small. To suggest that Sunday-schools are not needed by children above the poorest levels is snobbish nonsense. This moral rot which eats at the heart of our nation is at work at all levels.

(ii) Some parents, I have found, object to sending their children to Sunday-school because they like to take them out for the day on Sunday—or, at least, they want to go out for the day themselves, and the only way to secure that end is to take the children with them.

What are we to say to these parents?

Well, it is a question of priorities. If you carefully instruct your children in the faith—regularly, systematically—and give to it the thoroughness that you expect day-school teachers to give to their teaching, the omission of Sunday-school can be made up. But how many parents—be honest about it—give regular, systematic, and thorough teaching to their children about religion?

I have always supposed that a really devoted parent never asked, 'What do *I* want? What suits *me*?' but always 'What is best for my child?'

Well, what *is* best for the child; the cinema on a Sunday afternoon in the winter, and a ramble in the country on a Sunday afternoon in the summer . . . or, summer and winter, the strong, moral and spiritual teaching which is given in our Sunday-schools and in our Children's Church?

(iii) Some parents, with whom I have conversed on this subject, have adopted the superior air of the very broadminded, and seemed to imply that Sunday-schools were places where little bigots were made. 'I am teaching my children no religion,' they said. 'I am waiting until they grow up, and then they can form their own ideas for themselves.'

What do people mean when they say that they are giving their children no religious teaching, but allowing their children to form their ideas for themselves? Is there anything in this state of mind that we can respect?

It seems to me that they mean one of two things. They mean either:

(*a*) That they don't want their child made into what one might call a rigid denominationalist, believing that their branch of the Church is right, and *only* theirs; that those who worship Jesus Christ in other ways are all mistaken and their eternal destiny unsure.

They mean that . . . and, *if* they mean that, many of

us here, myself among them, would have a great sympathy with that point of view.

But that kind of teaching is *not* given in Sunday-schools today, or not in many, and in none that I know. There are people, of course, who are teaching children still that only *they* are right, and are, I suppose, in danger of manufacturing little bigots but, in the majority of Sunday-schools in this land—I affirm this quite positively —that kind of teaching is *not* given. The marrow of the gospel is given to the children, and they are never taught—in the majority of Sunday-schools—that those who worship our Lord in other ways are outside the pale.

Or (b)—and this is what I fear they *do* mean—they mean that they do not intend to give their children any religious teaching at all, but let them grow up, not even little pagans—because a pagan believed in a god of some sort—but little secularists into whose thought the super-natural never comes; who have no concept of reverence developed in their mind at all; who suppose that the universe is entirely materialistic and belongs to man and not to God, and whose ideas (quite often anaemic) of brotherly love, are buttressed with no spiritual sanc-tions at all.

I want to say it kindly, but plainly; I think this talk about leaving children to develop their own religious ideas is utter nonsense. How do you answer a child's deeper questions which begin to come even in his tender-est years? Do you really suppose that children can hold their minds in suspense through sixteen or seventeen years—the most formative years of their life—and then survey, as it were, the great religious figures of history and decide, in detachment, which one they'll choose? 'Shall it be Jesus, or the Buddha, or Mohammed, or Confucius, or Lao-tze . . . or shall I just worship science and sing my anthems to an atom bomb?'

It seems to me utterly foolish for people to think like that. Children have the right to the best that the race has learned in all the long development of humanity; the best in medicine and surgery; the best in hygiene and social welfare; the best in education; the best in everything. The best, therefore, in religion.

I say quite plainly, as a student of comparative religion for many years, that the best this world has ever learned about religion centres in Jesus Christ. I pay my willing tribute to whatever learning has come to our poor race by the illumination of great and good men everywhere. I speak with reverence of the holy books of other faiths: the Talmud, the Koran, the Analects, and all the rest of them, but God, who 'at sundry times and in divers manners' has spoken in time past by the sages of many religions, spoke at the last unto us by His Son, and that revelation supersedes all others.

Will you deny it, that children have a right to the best? Don't you honestly believe that the best of whom you've ever heard is Jesus Christ?

And I would say this also to those parents anxious to be broad-minded: 'Can't you be as "broad-minded" in other ways too? Why don't you leave your child to form his or her own ideas about manners until he is sixteen or seventeen? Why not allow him a similar independence in regard to social etiquette?'

You know, and I know, that if you taught a child no manners he'd make them on his own, and they would be pretty poor ones. So it is with spiritual values. If you leave a child without direction in regard to these most important things in life, he will get his own ideas, and they'll be pretty poor ones too. He will suppose that the world was made just for him. Egotism will guide his actions. Greed will be the key to a great deal of his conduct. Self will be in the centre of the picture most of the time.

K

A few years ago—nearly a generation now—a number of schools were started by advanced educationists the characteristic of which was that the child was never to be thwarted. Let the little darling do whatever he wanted—that was the principle. If he wanted to paint on the wall, he could. If he wanted to throw the ink-bottle at teacher, he could. The little child must *not* be repressed.

Well, enough time has gone by to see some of the beauties that system has produced, and we don't like them. Strangely enough, their parents don't like them either . . . nor even the people who started the schools!

It is dawning on some of these 'experts' that perhaps they were wrong; that there is that in human nature which needs to be disciplined and dealt with; that there might even be something, after all, in what the old theologians taught about original sin.

Yet the greatest sufferers from the neglect of religious instruction are the children themselves. To let them grow up without the gracious influence of Christ on their lives is pure tragedy, and a sin against their unformed natures.

'Feed my lambs,' said Jesus just before the Ascension. 'Feed my lambs.'

We, in the Church, want to take our share in fulfilling that injunction. The lambs are fed best in the home, but we are eager to co-operate with the home. I plead with any of you who are parents to take this counsel to heart, and I plead also with those of you who have influence on other parents to impress it upon them also.

15

He Confirms the Commandments

Mark 10¹⁷ᶠ—*Thou knowest the commandments.* . . .
Honour thy father and mother

THERE IS AN old—and in some ways an unimportant question—sometimes discussed by psychologists regarding the relationship of parent and child. It is this: 'Do parents love their children more than children love their parents, or is the excess of love on the side of the child?' There seems to be general agreement on the answer. Allowing for the exceptions which disturb every rule, it is usually agreed that parents *do* love their children more than the children love their parents, and this for several reasons.

First, they have a keener sense of possessiveness. Of all the emotions that fill these human hearts none is more intense than that which finds expression in the cry, 'My child'.

Secondly, they feel that their own life is being lived and tested again in the life of their offspring and consequently they have the profoundest sense of responsibility.

Furthermore, it is their task and privilege for many years to give and give and give (often to the point of sacrifice), while the child merely receives, and it is one of the curiosities of human nature that those who *give* usually feel more deeply than those who *receive*. Moreover, through the years of childhood, the parent's mind is so much bigger, and love and knowledge are curiously interwoven. Children are often blissfully unconscious of the sacrifices that are being made for them, and most people have to wait until they are parents themselves before they realize one-half of what their parents had so gladly done for them. It may not seem a very useful occupation to be weighing up the love of parent and child against child and parent. Indeed, the very inquiry may seem like a profane intrusion on an intimate relationship and yet it has a valuable purpose. I want to talk to you young men and women about our Lord's confirmation of the Commandments and in particular the Commandment, 'Honour thy father and thy mother.' There is no reciprocal Commandment exhorting parents to love or cherish their children. Such a Commandment would entrench far more on the unnatural than this one does. It is only the monstrosity among parents who fails to love and cherish the child, but it is not only the monstrosity among children who fails to honour father and mother. Young men who pass, among their friends, as 'jolly good fellows' are often guilty of it. Young women who are said to be 'awfully nice' are not seldom found wanting here. Let us look at this topic again. The Commandments are not a quaint survival of primitive ideas or Jesus would not have endorsed them; they are the fundamental moral axioms of all civilized life. I make no apology, therefore, on Youth Sunday, in exhorting you to honour your father and your mother. I recognize that one among you here or there may not have known their father or mother, and some even, who did know them, may not have had good parents, but to the great majority of you this is a plain word from heaven.

I

What does the word 'honour' mean in this connection. It means 'respect'—*profound* respect. The Hebrew word carried with it also the idea of obedience and service. There is no sense of inferiority in the word, but a great sense of filial duty. Ancient peoples laid much stress on these things. Sometimes indeed it was grossly exaggerated as in the ancestor worship of the Chinese, but the tendency today in the Western world is to underestimate its importance. Some young men find it hard to believe that a man can be old without being senile, and it is the fashion today to speak with contempt of anything 'Victorian'. The Chinese used to idolize their ancestors; we tend to apologize for ours. It is time we did a little clearer thinking on these matters.

There is no *mechanical* evolution in the realm of free men. One generation is not automatically better than the last. Men do not simply grow better than their fathers; if they are going to be better they must receive more grace. The evil things of this world do not just *come* right; they've got to be *put* right. And the finest starting-point in the crusade is a profound respect for the best that has been done before us.

II

Let us freely admit at this point that respect for, and obedience to, the wishes of one's elders is not always easy. Every generation as it comes has its own viewpoint, and asserts itself against its seniors. Customs and manners change also. Eighty years ago a man prepared to propose marriage by buying a large bunch of flowers, learning a speech (which often included some poetry), taking a deep breath, and setting out in the spirit of a sailor walking the plank. The girl prepared to receive him by rehearsing her swoon. He usually said something about placing his fortune at her feet, which she parried with the hint that it wasn't a very large fortune and he counterparried by declaring that beside her tiny feet it would look immense! Today all that patter is cut out. The proposal sometimes takes place over the telephone, and may be little more than 'Shall us? Let's.'

Personally, I dislike both ways, but it is some comment on the modern method that divorce is rapidly increasing and that, according to the latest book on the subject, the number of divorces in some countries is steadily approaching the actual number of marriages which are made. And there are usually a few years of misery before the case comes to court. It seems as though there was something to be said for the slower methods of other days.

Changes of outlook and custom are bound to affect the relationship of the generations. The old man thinks the young man is hasty and callow; the young man thinks the old man is hide-bound and conservative. This is one of the predisposing causes which sometimes accounts for the barrier between father and son. Nor is that barrier made less difficult to scale when the parents actually *do* make mistakes. The parents of Michelangelo declared that no son of theirs should be an artist. The father of Joshua Reynolds rebuked his son for drawing pictures, and wrote across one of them: 'Done by Joshua out of pure idleness.' Schiller and Goldsmith were sent to study surgery and Handel's father tried to kill his boy's love of music. They even tried to make J. M. W. Turner into a barber! The world knows now that all these were parental mistakes. Many others could be added to the list.

Nor are the mistakes of parents always confined to the choice of a child's profession. Sometimes they concern themselves with matters of the heart as well. All the world knows that Elizabeth Barrett eloped with Robert Browning and married him in the face of her father's fierce dissent. Yet it was one of the few happy marriages among the poets, and one of the choice love stories of the world.

My own Mother married Father in the face of strong

parental disapproval. They denied her a wedding reception, refused to come to the ceremony, and took a full year to get over their umbrage. Grandfather spent the eventide of his life playing with his grandsons and telling people what a foolish man he'd been.

Yes!—with all their love parents *do* sometimes make mistakes and it is in the full knowledge of that that I still persist in saying: 'Honour thy father and thy mother'.

III

What makes me so bold to persist in that point of view even when I have shown its possible errors?

I do so for these reasons:

First, because of the great love I mentioned as we began. It is a tremendous thing to run counter to a parent's sacrificial love. *Sometimes*, in the life of *some* people, it is necessary so to do, but it is a course to embark upon without any jauntiness and indeed with some pain.

Secondly, though I have shown that parents sometimes make mistakes, the plain truth is that they are usually right. The mistakes are the exceptions. They know the world. They know you. In the normal case their knowledge and love combine to produce right judgement. Thousands of young men and women have been saved from shipwreck by heeding parental advice and thousands more would have been saved had they not neglected it. I do not blame the father of Joshua Reynolds, or Michelangelo or Rembrandt van Rijn for opposing their sons' plans to become artists. It is still true that the average person who takes up fine art as a living discovers that it is a fine art to pay the rent! These fathers realized that. They were more modest than the multitudes of mothers who find it easy to believe that their child is a genius. They opposed the plan, and in these classic cases they were wrong. But they are not usually wrong. And even in these cases their opposition was not wholly profitless. It was a test of their son's sense of vocation. It was the means whereby the boy might determine whether he was moved by a passing whim or a profound sense of call. I say again, the hour *might* come in a young man or woman's life when they must disobey some parental command, but that hour (except in the rarest cases) cannot be before the years of discretion and even then it demands the closest thought.

IV

It is when we come to speak in detail of how a young man or young woman can honour father and mother that we encounter certain difficulties. In one sense the question never arises because, where love exists, the simple rule of life is just to do those things that will please one's parents and never to do those things that will grieve them. One might adapt a phrase of Augustine's and say, 'Love your parents and do what you like', because, if we really love them we wouldn't do anything to hurt them. And, if parents themselves were pressed to say what they wish, they would cast their requests into a negative rather than a positive mould. They would say in effect: 'Follow your bent—as long as it does not lead to things dishonourable. Do as you like—as long as it is useful and worthy, and to the glory of God.' In their generosity of heart, they would give us the widest freedom and help us to realize all our legitimate aspirations—as long as we cast no shadow on the honourable name they have given us, nor blot the family escutcheon which they have laboured to keep clean. No man can sin to himself—and no woman. Its shameful entail beats upon the parents who begot us. To any young man tempted to sin—to any young woman —I would say this: 'Think of what it involves for *them*. You may have weighed the consequences for yourself and be ready to face them, but you cannot weigh the consequences for your people. Think of them. Father is grey partly because of his efforts for you. You ploughed those lines in mother's face: when you were sick and she fought night and day to keep you alive and won. Are you going to run a plough across their hearts? It's no good talking about their 'old-fashioned morality'. Morality is one of the few things not subject to the law of fashion. The distinction between right and wrong is eternal and written in the heavens. There is no question of 'opinion' when it is covered by the Ten Commandments. Do the right thing! Honour thy father and thy mother!'

The best parents do not look upon their children as perpetual pensions. They have not educated you just with the idea that in their old age you will keep them. No! No! They want to avoid that. It is a dear hope of theirs never to be a drag upon you. They just want to see you forge ahead. It may be that the hour *will* come when they *do* need some help which you can give. That will be a *great* hour for you. You will be greedy for the privilege. With delicate courtesy and gentle unobtrusiveness you will meet that need and you will meet it in the manner of one deeply impressed with the privilege, and when you pray you will thank God that, though you can never pay them back, you have had the chance of illustrating how much you cared.

But, mark this! It is a privilege which will come to you without their will. The best of parents do not wish that. They want nothing from you but your love, and if you ask again what they mean by 'honour' they will say: 'Honour me by living a clean life. Honour God! Let me anticipate our family made complete again in Heaven.'

And, remember this, you can honour your parents in the hundred simple courtesies of daily life.

Some young men speak to their mothers with less

courtesy than they would use to a waitress. They come
in from work and say curtly: 'Where's my dinner?'
Where indeed? It is a common mistake of young people
at a certain age to think that their slight contribution to
the family income is really the mainstay of the home. It
very seldom is! It may hardly pay the electricity bill—
and if it was thrice the sum it would not justify that air of
arrogance. 'Honour thy father and thy mother!'

And mark you, if you fail to honour them, the day will
come when you will know the bitterness of vain regrets.

Samuel Johnson did. His father, you remember, was a
bookseller in Lichfield, but, on market days, he had a stall
in Uttoxeter too. One day he asked Sam to take care of the
stall—and Sam refused. His father was an eccentric
and a melancholiac, but this was sheer disobedience.

And do you remember, also, how his rudeness haunted
Sam through his later years? One day, long after his
father's death, he made his way to Uttoxeter and stood
bare-headed in the rain on the spot where his father's stall
once stood, as an act of penance for his rudeness and
disobedience more than half a century before.

Or—to take a more recent instance—think of Dick
Sheppard, the once-famous Vicar of St. Martin-in-the-
Fields. Dick Sheppard's father—himself a minor canon—
doted on his boy. Nothing pleased him so much as for
Dick to drop in for supper and a talk.

On the last evening of Dr Edgar Sheppard's life—
though no one had any idea that it was to be his last
evening—he kept postponing supper. 'Dick might come
in,' he said to his wife. And half an hour later: 'There's no
hurry, is there dear? Let's wait a while longer. Dick
might come in.'

Well, Dick didn't come, and they had supper, and that
night the minor canon moved on to a better choir than
he'd ever known.

Dick was almost inconsolable. He *could* have gone. A bit tired, maybe. . . . But he often said afterwards: 'I wonder if there is an angel who can take him a message that will tell him that, as the years go by, I am increasingly grateful to him. . . .'

Well . . . that is how you will feel if you neglect them, and have any sensitivity of conscience at all. 'I wonder if there is an angel . . .'

Save the angels the bother! Honour thy father and mother!

16

He Delights in Our Gratitude

Matthew 15³⁶— . . . *and he took the seven loaves and the fishes; and he gave thanks*

SO FAR AS thanksgiving is concerned, the mass of people can be divided into two classes: those who take things for granted and those who take things with gratitude.

It is my aim today to add to the number of those who take things with gratitude.

Notice, first, that it is the *right* thing to do. To take benefits from God or man without a thought or a word of thanks is mean, contemptible, and undermines faith in human nature. When a man has been treated by a fellow-man with ingratitude, the milk of human kindness curdles in him. He says afterwards, 'He never so much as said "Thank you". Even a dog would have wagged his tail.'

Not only is it the right thing to do: it is the *profitable* thing to do. Oh no, I am not thinking cynically, like Sir Robert Walpole, when he said that 'gratitude is a lively sense of future favours'. I don't mean 'profitable' in the sense that if you thank somebody you are more likely to get help from him again. I mean 'profitable' in the sense that a man who is quick to mark and swift to thank a kindness is in a constant state of happiness and goodwill. He has a barricade built against depression. He faces life buoyantly and confidently because he is aware of mercy streaming on him from Heaven and from his fellow-men as well.

So give thanks!

Jesus is our example in this as in all things. He was constantly giving thanks.

I admit that it isn't always easy to give thanks. 'How can you thank God for a cancer?' you might ask. Looked at like that, it is difficult, I know—though, in fact, the only people with cancer to whom I spoke last week both thanked God fervently for His mercies towards them. I am going to say this. To a Christian, even *this* quality of thanksgiving is gloriously possible. To those mature in the Christian faith, mercies can still be found near the heart of tragedy.

Oh, I know that there is a grotesque way of looking at it; a form of thanks which is not really thanks at all.

I heard the other day of a little girl—an unusual little girl in some ways and a naughty little girl as well—who detested milk pudding and had been made to eat some at her dinner. When she asked if she might get down from the table she was told to return thanks.

'But I have nothing to be thankful for,' she said sulkily.

'Very well,' said her mother. 'Remain there until you have.'

There was silence for a few minutes. Then a little voice said: 'Thank God I wasn't sick. *Now* may I get down?'

I need hardly say that that is not the freakish attitude of mind I am commending. Rather, it is this: If, as the Bible teaches, 'the steps of a good man are ordered by the Lord', a mature Christian will thank God even in trouble, the heaviest and most desolating trouble, that, though God did not 'lead' him into sickness, he is not deserted in it; that, though he cannot see it as yet, he has faith to believe that somewhere there is mercy at the heart of it, or good that can come out of it; that it is, indeed, only another of the 'all things' that still 'work together for good to them that love God'. The prayer of thanksgiving at such a time may, indeed, be what the Scriptures call a 'sacrifice of thanksgiving'; a thanksgiving that almost has blood upon it; an adoring venture of faith—believing in defiance of the God-denying look of things. But the mature will be able to offer even that: not easily but definitely. And the *sacrifice* of thanksgiving will be precious in God's sight.

Thank God that those times which strain faith so hard come only occasionally in life. For the most part we travel a sunlit road, and when we are unaware of the love of God it is often because we have not looked for it. To see the evidence of God's mercies you have only to look.

Let us look at them at this time of Harvest Festival; let us *stare* at them.

I

Let us begin with *the common blessings—so commonly overlooked*.

Let us thank God for the fecund earth. Not without toil and sweat and foresight and struggle have all these lovely things been drawn from the earth. God did not set us in the world to receive our food merely by wishing for it. It comes only by the sweat of someone's brow, but the sweat alone would be useless without the added blessing of God. Look, I say, at this wonderful display, and, for all the kindly fruits of earth, be grateful.

Let us thank God for our five senses and for whatever measure of health we enjoy.

I met a depressed man one day who told me that he had nothing to be thankful for, so I said: 'Well, I'm going visiting; come with me.'

I was going to the Institution for the poor aged sick. In the town where I then ministered it was an old-fashioned building, and its management left much to be desired; but the man came with me. It was not a public visiting day, but I got him in 'on the nod', and he just

came round the wards with me. From bed to bed we
went, seeing a great many of these pitiable old people.
Some were dim of sight, and some were *quite* blind. Some
were hard of hearing, and some were *quite* deaf. Some
were imbecile, and in some their reason was *partly* im-
paired. (They seemed almost the most pitiable cases of
all because, in their lucid moments, they knew the truth
about themselves, and that was hard to bear.)

I didn't say anything much to my companion. I had
come to visit the poor souls themselves; he just followed
me round.

When we were outside again I did not rub the moral
in. I just shook hands with him, because I had other
duties to do, and he parted from me saying: 'I don't
think I'll ever grumble again.'

It was a simple device; just showing him people less
fortunate than himself. He went away saying (I think)
under his breath, 'I can see. I can see the face of my
dear ones. I can see the sunshine and the first flowers
which come out from the hard, dark earth in the Spring.

'I can hear. I can hear the song of birds; the blackbirds
fluting in the orchard and the carefree laughter of little
children.

'I have my reason unimpaired. I can think and plan
and pray. I am not well off, but I have enough. I have
a roof over my head, and food that I have bought on my
table. I have, at least, a little in reserve against a rainy
day. . . .'

Almost (not quite), but almost every single soul in this
church now can see and hear, and all of you (so far as I
know) have your reason utterly unimpaired. Thank
God for the common blessings commonly overlooked.
Don't wait till you lose them to be grateful. Look about
you now at this harvest display; think of the fruitful earth,
the solid structure of the seasons, the framework of the

universe shaped in love and given to men. These are common blessings if you like, and yet, if you lost them and could know your loss, you would give almost all the other things you have to recover them and marvel, in your deprivation, that when you had them you did not value them more.

Thank God for common blessings; for the harvest fully gathered in and the great harvest moon rising above; for the sudden smile of a friend met unexpectedly in a place where you did not expect to meet anyone you knew; thank God for home, for birthday anniversaries, for the bulge and mystery of stockings in the dark on Christmas morning; thank God for the loyalty of the family when they laugh at your old joke, told the fiftieth time, but tried out expectantly on the new guest; for all ordinary things, taken for granted when they ought to be taken with gratitude: Thank God! Thank God!

II

First, thanks to God for the common blessings, commonly overlooked; secondly, thanks to God for *the special blessings—soon, alas, forgotten*.

Special blessings? Yes, we have had them. We have *all* had them. You may not have recognized them as such at the time, but they were. I suppose it is more probable, however, that you *did* half-recognize them, but you forgot them so soon.

God never gives a blessing just for the hour. Every special blessing is not only for the hour itself, but for the future. It is a pledge; it is as though God were to say, 'I'll do this for you now, and then you will *always* know that you are the object of My love.'

What a sad thing it is, therefore, that we forget so soon. That is why new dangers can startle you with fear and dismay. You have forgotten the past mercies. You would have been calm and confident in the presence of this new trouble if you had remembered vividly the old deliverance; if you had kept it fresh in mind and been able to say, 'The God who delivered me then didn't deliver me then to desert me now.' And yet you are fearful in the presence of this new possibility and might be as ignorant as some savage in the mid-most forest who did not know that he had a loving Father in Heaven.

Remember old John Newton?—

> *His love in time past forbids me to think*
> *He'll leave me at last in trouble to sink.*

St Teresa was in a mood of deep depression one day. Saint though she was, I think she had forgotten for an hour the many deliverances that God had vouchsafed to her. So God came and said, 'When did I ever fail thee? I am today what I have always been.'

Make a practice of noting your special blessings. Be as thorough about it as a missionary I read about who was a most diligent man in prayer and a master of 'method' too. He used to note carefully in little books the special blessings he received and the answers he had to his prayers. The little books are still preserved, I believe. On the last day of the year he would assess the answers. There were usually between 87 and 90 per cent of plain, impressive answers to the prayers which he had offered, and even concerning the rest he would not have admitted that they had not been answered. He would have said about those: 'In regard to these things, for some purpose known to my Father, the answer had to be "Wait" or "No".'

Make a practice of thanking God for His goodness to you and thanking those also by whose hand the blessing came. It does people good to be thanked. It is amazing what you will do for others, as well as for your own soul, if you will follow this counsel of saying a sincere 'Thank you'.

Let me put that last point in a picture for you.

When the business depression in America was at its worst, a group of men sat in a room talking over the sad state of affairs, and one of them was a friend of mine, a Methodist minister, the Rev. Professor William L. Stidger of the School of Theology in Boston, Massachusetts. The conversation concerned the recession in trade and got more miserable every moment it went on. But as Thanksgiving Day was near—a great day in America —a minister present said, 'I have got to preach on Thanksgiving Day. I want to say something affirmative. What can I say that is affirmative in a period of world depression like this?'

Stidger began to think of the blessings he had had in life and the things for which he was truly thankful. He remembered the woman who had taught him in the infants' school, and of whom he had not heard for many years. Although it was the *infants'* school, he still remembered that she had gone out of her way to put a love of verse in him, and Stidger has loved verse all his life. So he wrote a letter of thanks to the old lady. This is the reply he had. It was written in the feeble scrawl of the old, and it began 'My dear Willie'. He was thrilled about that. Stidger was over fifty at the time and bald and a professor, and he didn't think there was anybody left in the world who would call him 'Willie'. It made him feel years younger right off. Here is the letter. I'll give it to you word for word:

My dear Willie,

I cannot tell you how much your note meant to me. I am in my eighties, living alone in a small room, cooking my own meals, lonely and, like the last leaf of autumn, lingering behind.

You will be interested to know that I taught in school for fifty years and yours is the first note of appreciation I ever received. It came on a blue-cold morning and it cheered me as nothing has in many years.

Stidger is not sentimental, but he wept over that note. Stidger thought of other people who had been kind to him. He remembered one of his old bishops who had been most helpful at the beginning of his ministry. The bishop was in retirement and had recently lost his wife. Stidger wrote a belated letter of thanks to the bishop. This was the reply:

My dear Will,

Your letter was so beautiful, so real, that as I sat reading it in my study, tears fell from my eyes; tears of gratitude. Then, before I realized what I was doing, I rose from my chair and called her name to show it to her—forgetting for a moment that she was gone. You will never know how much your letter has warmed my spirit. I have been walking about in the glow of it all day long.

Need I say anything more? I want you to make a practice of thanking people; of taking a little trouble to thank them. It will please God. He often sends His special mercies by the hands of other people. He *normally* does. I think He likes His agent to be thanked also. Here is a resolution to be made at the time of Harvest Festival. Give thanks! Give Thanks!

III

First, the common blessings commonly overlooked; secondly, the special blessings soon forgotten; thirdly, the greatest blessing—tragically ignored.

What is the greatest blessing? Oh, there is no doubt about that. Paul was quite a master of words and he seldom found that they failed him, but there *was* a subject on which words fell short, and on one occasion, when it came to his mind, he said: 'Thanks be to God for his unspeakable gift.'

Note that word 'unspeakable'. Paul was saying, in effect: 'It just won't go into words.'

What was so wonderful that it wouldn't go into words? What had the Father given for which no thanks were really adequate?

The gift of Jesus Christ! *He* was the unspeakable gift. Thanks be to God (above everything else), says Paul, for *Him*.

I have often sat down and meditated on what my life would have been, without Christ. It is a dark picture. Poor as I know my life still to be, I dare hardly think of it apart from Him. When Baron von Hügel considered the same question, he said of the religion of Jesus:

I should not be physically alive at this moment; I should be, were I alive at all, a corrupt or at least an incredibly unhappy, violent, bitter, self-occupied destructive soul, were it not for religion and for its having come and saved me from myself— it, and nothing else, it, in a sense, against everything else.

All this he felt about the power of Christ in his life. I would phrase it differently, but my own honest witness would be no less emphatic than his. I believe every good thing in my life came from God and—if any doubter wanted to wipe that aside as nothing but an act of faith —I would go farther and say that I can actually *trace* most of them. My deepening conviction that divine love is the only satisfying motive in life, my life's partner, my blissfully happy home, the love of child and friend, the joy of service . . . they all came as smaller gifts in the hand of 'the unspeakable Gift'—from Christ Himself.

Nor are the blessings only personal. When I see this dark world through His eyes, I have hope for it. When I feel the pulse of His power re-moulding my own stubborn nature, I know what He can do with all men. When I see His clear reflection in the saints—in men and women who have given Him the fullest opportunity—I know again that He is the Saviour of the world.

Yet multi-millions who know of Him, ignore Him; deny His world-wide and all-time significance; assert that this world belongs to us who never called it into being nor understand how it works; spurn the 'unspeakable gift' as a figment of our child minds. . . .

Be wiser than they are! At this time of thanksgiving—thanksgiving for the harvest, but much more than the harvest—thank God for His 'unspeakable gift' in whose hand every other precious thing comes as well.

One of the worst moments for an atheist is when he feels thankful and has no One to thank! You are not in that position! You thank the Father for the Son, and both for the Holy Spirit. To trace every 'good and perfect gift' to its true source—the Father of Light—is a good thing; it keeps one orientated to the Highest; it maintains the concept of reverence in our minds without which every mortal mind is deficient; it reminds us who is in charge.

I conclude with this:

We are often rebuked in our thanklessness by people less fortunate than we are ourselves and we are often reminded by them of the number and source of our blessings.

Here is an instance. A ministerial friend of mine used to visit an invalid girl. She was a devout person. One of her several sicknesses was a tendency to curvature of the spine and she lived in a Phelp's box. Have you ever seen a Phelp's box? It looks like a shallow coffin—a grisly anticipation of the grave—and children with a tendency to curvature of the spine used to be strapped in one, as nearly flat as possible.

Her box was by the window, and she said to my friend one day:

'In this position I can only look up. On those nights when I can't sleep, I play with the stars.'

'Play with the stars?' he asked. 'How can you play with the stars?'

'This way,' she said. 'I pick out the brightest star I can find and I say: "That's Mummy." I pick out another bright one, and say: "That's Daddy." I find a twinkling one for my brother, my puppy, my spinal perambulator . . .' on and on she went. Nothing seemed forgotten. Then she concluded with this:

'But there aren't enough stars to go round!'

There aren't enough stars to go round!

Go home, you thankless people, and count the stars!

17

He Claims the Whole World

Matthew 28¹⁹—*Make disciples of all nations*

LAST WEEK, my wife went into a shop and, in the course of her business, it transpired that she had a daughter who was a missionary in India.

'I don't believe in missionaries,' said the woman in charge of the shop.

'And why?' asked my wife.

'I don't believe', said the shopkeeper, 'that we have any right to go into other countries interfering with them.'

'I DON'T BELIEVE THAT WE HAVE ANY RIGHT TO GO INTO OTHER COUNTRIES INTERFERING WITH THEM.'

That was what she said. If that was only *her* opinion, I wouldn't be mentioning it here in the pulpit; but it isn't!

Hundreds of thousands of people in this country believe just that. It may be millions. They *pride* themselves on believing it. They think that they are advanced, broad-minded, and superior to entertain those views. Missionary work, by implication, is the occupation of bigots.

We had better examine this elementary question again.

I propose to do it this way.

We often think of human beings as comprised of body, mind and soul. The distinction must not be pressed too far, but it is a useful one. All three aspects of our nature are interrelated, of course. A man's mind is not separate from his body, like the kernel of a nut from its shell. The difference between the mind and the soul is not easily and firmly drawn. But we know roughly what we mean by those three parts of our nature. This body —the flesh and blood of me, with its five senses relating me to the physical world. This mind—with which I reason and plan and hope and know. The soul in me— by which I aspire to God, and reach out beyond all bounds of time and space, and seek fellowship with the life at the heart of the universe.

Body, mind and soul!

Wherever you meet humanity, you meet body, mind and soul.

Missionary work is directed to the whole man and woman, so let us look at it in those three aspects of body, mind and soul.

I

Some people—usually those who have never lived abroad—have idyllic pictures of life overseas. They have got their ideas from highly coloured pictures, from films, and from novels; indeed, from anywhere but from personal experience.

In this land of their imagination, the sun is always shining and yet there is always a cool breeze too. Work is unnecessary. The hut practically keeps itself clean. Everybody is simple and kind. There are no snakes or wild animals; no germs; no disease; plenty of servants, and nothing to do all day long but lie in the sun, and, when you want a meal, you put up your hand and take the luscious fruit from the trees, and everything is perfect in this best of all possible worlds—*until a missionary turns up and interferes with it all*. It really looks as though we need a Society for the Suppression of Missionary Societies!

Well, that is the imagination! What are the facts?

Here is an extract from a letter received recently from an honest reporter in a village in Hyderabad, South India. Perhaps I should say (like the advertiser says) that the original letter can be seen on application.

We arrived in the village in an old car at late afternoon. It was a jumbly mass of little mud huts without any pathways. . . . At each hut a few children came out and tagged behind us as we walked around. Most of the children were naked, though a few had a rag on. All had sores, running noses, and verminous heads. Our first child was covered with the most terrible oozing wounds and his head a mass of scabs. Sheila explained to me that it is common to brand a child of that age (three) in order that the intense pain suffered will drive the spirit of pain away from the body for ever. The smells, the diseases, the deformities, the filth made me so sick I didn't think I could prevent myself from vomiting. I made myself take the stump of an arm of one little child who had no hand and I watched the insects in her hair as we walked along together. . . .

In the end, we took about fifty children to a flat piece of muddy ground and, by the light of a single hurricane lamp, organized games for them. There was no real gaiety, because children here are born old and with too much knowledge. But some interest crept into a few faces, and they danced round in a ring like old people playing at being young again.

When I think of all the books I have read about the glamour and mystery of the East, I want to jam them down their authors' throats. It is unrelieved hell, and (in a moment of weakness) I thought there was nowhere else on earth that I would not rather be.

Now that, I believe, is honest reporting. It was not written by a lady novelist in London, nor even by somebody living in semi-state in Kashmir. Disease is prevalent among primitive peoples. It is an illusion that man, in what is called 'the natural state', is free of disease. The first people from the West to reach New

Zealand found the fine Maori race quite in the primitive state and decimated by T.B.! The pain, the suffering, and most of the diseases we know (and many we do not know) are there in the East crying aloud for Western medicine and Western skill.

Do you call it 'interfering' to put a hospital down in the midst of that ocean of need? Are you going to call the missionary doctor a 'busy-body' who gives his life to work like that and gets only bread and cheese for doing it when he might be practising his profession in comfort at home, and being not ungenerously paid for it by the State? If that is interference, all the suffering millions of the East would cry out: 'Interfere with us more.'

In Great Britain, there is one doctor for every 840 members of the community. In India, there is one doctor for every 6,500 members of the community.

In Great Britain, there is one nurse to every 240 members of the community. In India, there is one nurse to every 43,000.

Notice that: 240; 43,000.

But don't let us interfere with them! *We* are all right. We get three meals a day, and the health services, and education, and this and that. They have one meal a day, and millions of them have practically no health service and no education, despite the fine efforts of the Indian Government to put it right. But don't let us interfere with them!

Is that broad-mindedness? It is downright selfishness, and we might as well call it by its right name.

II

I turn from the ministry to the body to the ministry of the mind.

You notice in that letter from Hyderabad that a little boy of three was deliberately branded that the intense pain suffered would drive the spirit of pain away from his body for ever.

What a grotesque idea! How had it ever happened that a mother should submit her own dear child to such inhuman torture? Didn't she love him?

Oh yes! She loved him. Indian mothers are devoted mothers. She loved him enough to lay down her life for him. But that is what she had been *taught*: that if she inflicted pain on her child to that intense degree he would be emancipated from pain afterwards.

It is the fruit of false religious teaching, and it had gone into her mind and led to conduct as awful as that.

And those ideas are not easily removed from the mind. You cannot wipe it out with a word. They *believe* it. They believe it deeply. It is part of their religion, and you must not interfere with people's religion. Let them put their own babies through all the horrors of hell, but you mustn't interfere with their religion. That is bigotry! The broad-minded will be against you!

Now, to get those wrong ideas out of the minds of people is a long and difficult business. It is the business of the teacher. Teaching is—God knows—a serious profession. People make fun of teaching at times and say with Bernard Shaw: 'He who can—does; he who can't—teaches.'

We can laugh at that (and none laughs louder than the teacher himself), but we still esteem their high calling. Thank God for teachers who hear the call of God to the overseas field. They go to minister to the minds of people; to teach them the wrong, among other things, of branding little children of three, out of a twisted devotion which could be kind in its intention, but is hideous in its results.

We have all been reading of the Mau-Mau atrocities in Kenya. Let us leave aside, for the moment, the perplexing political and economic aspects of this—though they can't be left aside indefinitely. The thing, as we see it, is awful and hideous. It over-simplifies it to call it an 'anti-white movement'. More loyal Kikuyu than Europeans were murdered by the Mau-Mau. Mau-Mau is a satanic thing in many of its expressions. There is a kind of ritual behind it. These murderers use *mpangas*, or long knives, and they slash the bodies of their victims in a symbolic way.

A friend of mine is a planter in Kenya. He has gathered the remains of many of these slaughtered people, Europeans and Kikuyu as well. I cannot tell you from the pulpit things he has told me in his letters, but the symbolic character of this deadly slashing is quite plain. Always the wrists of the victims are slashed, and particularly the left wrist. What evil and muddled ideas lie behind that, we do not know. Little children, as you know, are slashed to pieces too.

There is some hazy meaning in the mixed-up minds of these murderers, half-revealed and half-concealed by the way they hack at a human body. They are bound by some terrible oath. When loyal servants have turned on their kind employers and been interrogated afterwards on why they did that awful thing, they have said: 'I didn't *want* to do it. My master was always kind to me, but the power of the oath was too strong.'

You see? It is bound up, in some way, with a debased religion. Their half-awakened minds are in the grip of the occult. Many of these people are in dread of the witch-doctor, and they do things from a superstitious compulsion from which, as yet, they cannot break free.

I do not know the answer to this—except wise Christian teaching. Somehow—and it will take years—it has to be imparted to the minds of these people that the great God of the universe is not a murderous devil, but the loving Father whom Jesus Christ revealed; that the Ten Commandments are the basis of all morality; that our Lord's commandments have to be added to them; that all people are sinners and need a Saviour, and that some of the white people who have gone to live among them are not good examples of the religion they profess. Indeed, some of them have been a shocking contradiction of it.

What an immense, and patient, and important task it is to minister to the minds of people. Is it not clear that the teacher must take his place with the doctor and the nurse, or else the task is incomplete? Is it not clear enough that to describe this ministry to the minds of benighted people as 'interference' is utterly to misconceive the whole thing?

III

I turn, finally, to the souls of men. We have seen the need to minister to the body; we have seen the need to minister to the mind.

Some people would call a halt there.

'No more,' they would say. 'We see no need for the evangelist to join the missionary team. Doctors, nurses, teachers, if you like, but not evangelists.'

Well, let us look at it again. I said, as I began, that the difference between the mind and the soul is not easily and firmly drawn, and that has come out in our inquiry. The task of the teacher impinged on the task of the evangelist again and again.

When you face the problem of that branded child— and there will be many thousands like him; when you face the problem of the Mau-Mau and a whole colony in unrest and fear . . . it is not just secular teaching which will meet the problem. Three R's cannot cure that. Writing, reading and arithmetic fall short of the goal. German, geometry and geography won't touch the heart of it. It is wrong religion that lies behind it, and only God's religion will put it right.

People unread in comparative religion like to say: 'One

religion is as good as another.' It sounds broad-minded. Actually, it is a judgement of ignorance.

There are fine things in the Moslem faith. The Moslem faith has its saints. Mohammed himself was, in his age, a great reformer.

There are fine things in the philosophy of Hinduism. There is noble, ethical teaching in the writing of Confucius. There are things in Buddhism beautiful indeed.

Christianity recognizes these fine things and blesses God for them, but Christianity says, if I may adapt the opening words of the Epistle to the Hebrews: 'God, who at sundry times and in divers manners spake in time past unto the fathers by the prophets (and by these Eastern sages), hath, in these last days, spoken unto us by his Son.'

That is our claim. Not that other world religions contain in them nothing of value. God forbid! But that they were not God's last word to His people.

Christianity is not one religion among others. It is in a category by itself.

We have, in this materialistic age, much in common with all who are theists, and we are glad to work with them against militant atheism; but we claim for the religion of Jesus Christ that it is unique, unsurpassed, and unparalleled; the word not of a prophet, but of the Son himself.

No other world faith even claims that its great teacher was God Incarnate. We claim for Christ that—as God —He meets every human need. He comes from the highest and He comes all the way. He meets us where we are, and He does the work. There is no human need outside His power to meet. Every spiritually sensitive man is aware of guilt and aware that, alone, he can do nothing about it. Christ atoned for sin and can forgive it. Every normal man is in awe of death and can't escape it. Christ conquered death and has opened the way to eternal life. His call is to all humanity. He abides no barriers of race, class or colour. 'Whosoever will may come.' It seems, to the devotees of other faiths, intolerant on the part of Christians to refuse to allow Jesus to go into a pantheon. How can they? Believing what they do about Him, they cannot concede even by implication that there are any 'gods' or prophets equal to Him. He is unique in His Person, in His Mission, and in His finished work.

Christianity is not a Western religion forced on the East. It is, in its origin, an Eastern religion, but in its nature it is a world faith. It is no more mine and yours than China's, India's, Africa's. It is God's provision for man, as man, and knows no barrier at all. To say that one religion is as good as another is to speak without knowledge of the subject we referred to just now as 'comparative religion'.

What is the best way to treat a wound in your body— a gash, say, on your forearm? People in one part of the world say that the best way to deal with a wound like that is to cover it with cow-dung. Some superstitious people in our own country, years ago, used to treat wounds with what they called 'sympathetic powder'. They left the wound alone, but anointed the weapon which caused the wound with a certain powder, and, as the wound healed by nature's own unhindered work, the recovery was attributed to the powder reposing on the knife. Still other people believe that the way to heal a wound quickly is to have a lucky charm on your person, which will probably prevent you getting hurt at all, but, if you do, will make you well very soon. Most of us believe today that to apply some antiseptic to the wound and keep it free of dirt is the best thing of all.

Now, of course, a person who knew little about healing, but knew that all those methods were employed in different places for the treatment of a wound, could say, if he liked: 'They are all *equally* good. Please yourself! There are people who believe in each of those four methods and have believed in them for a long time.' He might *say* that—especially if he traded in lucky charms!

But we know that that is all nonsense. They are *not* equally good. The last is the best.

It is something like that, that I am seeking to say about the faith it is my privilege to proclaim. The whole world has a right to the best which any one part of the world has learned. The best the world has learned about religion centres in Jesus Christ. It is not 'interfering' to take His faith into all the world. It is plain humanity to do so.

If they discovered the cure of cancer in Russia and kept the secret behind the 'iron curtain', it would be a sin against humanity. If they discovered the cure of cancer in America and tried to keep it in the Western world, it would be a sin against humanity. If we, to whom it has pleased God to reveal Himself in Jesus Christ, were to keep the knowledge of Christ to ourselves, it would be a sin against humanity.

Jesus said, 'Make disciples of all nations,' and His command itself were reason enough for missionary work. But His command is reinforced by the unspeakable need of people throughout the wide earth. Not because we are shining examples ourselves of His way of life; not because we are unmindful of light which has come by other lamps; not because we are personally superior to those who worship in other ways, but because *He* is the Light of the World and utterly indispensable, we claim the whole world in His Name.